The Role of the Suprem
Court in American Politics

Dilemmas in American Politics

Series Editor   **L. Sandy Maisel,** *Colby College*

Dilemmas in American Politics offers teachers and students a series of quality books on timely topics and key institutions in American government. Each text will examine a "real world" dilemma and will be structured to cover the historical, theoretical, policy relevant, and future dimensions of its subject.

The Role of the Supreme Court in American Politics

The Least Dangerous Branch?

Richard L. Pacelle, Jr.
University of Missouri–St. Louis

A Member of the Perseus Books Group

Library
University of Texas
at San Antonio

Copyright © 2002 by Westview Press, A Member of the Perseus Books Group

Westview Press books are available at special discounts for bulk purchases in the United States by corporations, institutions, and other organizations. For more information, please contact the Special Markets Department at the Perseus Books Group, 11 Cambridge Center, Cambridge MA 02142, or call (617) 252-5298.

Published in 2002 in the United States of America by Westview Press, 5500 Central Avenue, Boulder, Colorado 80301–2877, and in the United Kingdom by Westview Press, 12 Hid's Copse Road, Cumnor Hill, Oxford OX2 9JJ

Find us on the World Wide Web at www.westviewpress.com

A C.I.P. catalog record for this book is available from the Library of Congress
0-8133-6753-0 (pbk)

The paper used in this publication meets the requirements of the American National Standard for Permanence of Paper for Printed Library Materials Z39.48-1984.

10   9   8   7   6   5   4

To Harriet K. Kral and the memory of Stanley K. Kledaras for their boundless support, kindness, generosity, and humor.

Contents

1 The Supreme Court: Law or Politics?   7

2 The Historical Dimension of the Dilemma   33

3 The Democratic Dimension of the Dilemma: Unelected Policymaking 51

4 The Institutional Dimension of the Dilemma: Constitutional and Self-Imposed Limitations 77

5 The Judicial Capacity Dimension of the Dilemma: Does the Supreme Court Have the Ability to Make Policy? 105

Illustrations

Figures

Tables

Acknowledgments

I SENT THE MANUSCRIPT to the editors before Thanksgiving 2000, never dreaming that the U.S. Supreme Court would intervene in the presidential election and force me to rewrite portions of the last chapter. The Court's role in the controversy did increase the attention of my students. Every 124 years or so, when the electoral process has a major hemorrhage, is a great time to be a political scientist.

I want to thank the students from my Honors Judicial Decision Making class and my Proseminar in Public Law. Although they did not always know it, I often bounced ideas off them. The former class, a simulation of the Supreme Court, had the opportunity to accept a version of *Bush v. Gore* and denied the "writ." I gave each of the "justices" an A that day. My graduate seminar students, particularly Brandon Bartels, Bill Perkins, and Marc Hendershot, helped me conceptualize "legitimacy" and "capacity." Andrea Pyatt, my research assistant, helped with a lot of background information and in preparing the manuscript.

I want to thank Professors Craig Rimmerman and David Canon for their suggestions, which made the final product better. Craig is an old friend and excellent teacher, and I respect his comments about how this book would read and be used in class. I have never met Professor Canon, but I hope this thanks will suffice until I do. His comments, particularly about the first chapter, helped me sharpen my focus. I also want to thank an anonymous reviewer, a public law expert apparently, who had pages of suggestions and saved me from some errors. I incorporated most of the suggestions, but the brevity of the book meant I had to neglect a few. My colleague Bryan Marshall generously offered to read revised versions of a number of chapters and provided valuable suggestions.

I owe an enormous debt to Professor Sandy Maisel, the Dilemma series editor, and Leo Wiegman, the Westview Press editor. They were very patient with me when I was a little slow getting the first draft to them and very helpful in distilling the reviewers' comments, encouraging me throughout the project. They have been a pleasure to work with at every stage. This was the last book for Leo at Westview; he left during the book's final stages. I did not initially think that I was the cause, until David Pervin left weeks after taking over as editor. David was very helpful in getting the manuscript ready for publication. I thank Barbara Greer for taking over the project and promising not to leave Westview before it was completed.

I appreciate the efforts of Steve Catalano who guided me through the production process. I owe a great debt to Susan Hindman, the copy editor. She had her work cut out for her and saved me from a number of errors. Original artwork was provided by a fantastic young artist, Laura Gunther. I have an original Gunther in the west wing of my home, which I am certain is worth a lot more now.

I have a number of long-term debts to acknowledge. Jan Frantzen and Lana Vierdag of the Political Science Department at the University of Missouri–St. Louis have made my life so much easier in so many ways. Professor Larry Baum, who read parts of the manuscript, has been a tireless supporter and friend since 1979. I was fortunate and smart enough to study under his direction. He has been a great role model.

While each of these individuals played a role in making this book better, I bear all responsibility for errors of commission or omission. I ask for a little indulgence and latitude in this endeavor. Writing a book for a general audience is not an easy task. In addition, there are some complex concepts for author and student alike to wrestle with. I had to take some liberties being brief in places to make general points. This is not an exhaustive analysis of the Supreme Court. Having said that, I assume full responsibility for the content. My eyes are open for any swinging two-by-fours.

A few personal notes. I cannot possibly express all that Fenton Martin has done for me and all that she means to me. I suppose everyone who writes a book owes a great deal to his or her spouse or significant other. My debt is enormous. Beyond her love, support, patience, the occasional kick in the pants, and willingness to listen to my ideas (too few) and complaints (too many), as a political science librarian she provides me with an in-house source of reference and research answers. As a published author of guides and bibliographies about matters far and wide— but most important, about the Supreme Court—she is an expert "who kindly endures my odd questions." Fenton graciously read chapters and offered a number of suggestions.

I want to thank my stepsons, Russell and Craig, for listening to my stories, talking politics and law with me, and just being great. The same does not go for Jackson and Hugo, whose wanting to go out and come in and go out and come in slowed down completion of this project. At least, that is my story and I am sticking to it.

I want to take this opportunity to acknowledge members of my family for their support and inspiration. I come from a long line of teachers. My father; Aunts Harriet Kral, Cally Angeletti, and Dorothy Guiliotis; Uncle Joe Angeletti; and my sisters, Kim Johnsky and Wendy Hathaway—as well as my best friend, Ed Mongillo—are educators at different levels. They have each taught me by example that teaching is a noble enterprise. In many ways, I guess I just went into the family business.

It is not supposed to be this way because I am the oldest, but I look up to my brother Wayne, the vice president of the Humane Society of the United States, and my sisters, one an assistant principal and the other the director of a day care center. I take great comfort in the fact that I am the least successful member of the family. We certainly owe a great deal to our parents, and I thank them for their support and love. They deserve a large measure of the credit for our successes.

I respectfully dedicate this book to one of those teachers, my aunt, Harriet Kral, and to the memory of my uncle, Stanley Kledaras, who was not a teacher but taught me a great deal. Both of them served as extra parents to my brother, sisters, and cousins. On behalf of all of them, I want to express my gratitude. Aunt Harriet cultivated and encouraged my early interest in books and current events. She has been an endless source of support in every form. I miss Uncle Stan, who was my benefactor in every possible way. Not a day goes by that I do not think about the profound effect the two of them had on me and all that I owe them.

R.L.P.

Introduction: A Five-Week Election Night Ends Up in the Supreme Court

．．．

L ET ME START BY apologizing to my former students. Since I began teaching American politics and the judicial process as a graduate student in 1981, I have taught students that the president of the United States selected the justices who serve on the U.S. Supreme Court. So imagine my surprise when in December 2000, the justices of the Supreme Court selected the president. Well, at least it seemed that way.

If this were a novel or a movie, it would be considered unbelievable and would be panned by the critics. An American election is too close to call for more than a month. One state hangs in the balance—and that state is governed by the brother of one of the candidates. The person who has to certify the final election results is a partisan who was the cochair of that candidate's state campaign for president. Further complicating the equation, that candidate's father had been the country's president and was a past director of the Central Intelligence Agency. But I'm getting ahead of the story.

On November 7, 2000, Americans went to the polls. Shortly after most of the polls in Florida closed (some in the state's panhandle were still open), first one television network, then another, and then the rest colored the state blue to designate that Democratic candidate Vice President Al Gore had won its twenty-five electoral votes. Within a half-hour, Michigan and Pennsylvania were also colored blue and for all the world, it appeared that Gore was well on his way to keeping the White House in Democratic hands. Governor George W. Bush, watching the returns with his family in Texas, was mortified. His pollsters had assured him that he was going to prevail. Thickening the plot further was the fact that George W.'s brother, Jeb, was the governor of Florida. Jeb left the family dinner to work the phones. He told his older brother that the night was still young and the final returns would place the state in the Republican fold.

Around 10:30, the networks recanted: One by one, they changed the color of Florida from blue to neutral, indicating a toss-up again. Hours after many Americans were in bed, the networks turned Florida red, meaning the state had gone to Bush, and declared him the winner of the presidency. Supporters in front of the governor's mansion in Austin celebrated. Gore, in his home state of Tennessee, was driving to his campaign headquarters to give his concession speech. Meanwhile, the numbers were changing: Bush's lead in the real returns from Florida was tightening by the moment. Suddenly, again, it was too close to call, and the networks again backed away from their projections. Gore, who had conceded to Bush on the phone, placed a second call to rescind his concession. American politics was about to move into uncharted territory.

Florida law required an automatic recount because of the close margin. If it is possible to conceive, things got even more tangled. The American public learned a whole new vocabulary: "hanging chads," "pregnant chads," and "dimpled chads." The public, suddenly enthralled with politics, watched the proceedings. It was clear by the election results—an evenly split Senate, a closely divided House, and the presidential popular vote—that there was a great deal of discord in the nation. The wrangling divided the public still further. Foreign observers had a bit of fun at America's expense. Some referred to America as a "banana republic." Fidel Castro offered to send election observers from Cuba to preside over the recount.

But this is not a book about the election of 2000. Democrats and Republicans sent former Secretaries of State William Christopher and James Baker to the Sunshine State. They were followed by legions of attorneys and observers. When hundreds of lawyers descend on an area, can use of the courts be far behind? Many state courts got involved, as attorneys for Bush sued to certify the results and end the election, while attorneys for Gore sued to recount all the votes. The Florida Supreme Court, with all seven judges appointed by Democrats, eventually interceded and unanimously gave Gore a big victory, saying, in effect, that all the votes in Florida should be counted.

The Bush legal team appealed the decision to the U.S. Supreme Court, arguing that the Florida Supreme Court had overstepped its bounds and was exhibiting *judicial activism*. Most analysts felt that the justices of the U.S. Supreme Court would demonstrate *judicial restraint* and simply refuse to accept the case. The justices confounded the experts by accepting the case and remanding it to the Florida Supreme Court for reevaluation. After a separate lower court decision favorable to Bush, the Florida Supreme Court, by a closer vote, essentially reinstated its initial ruling, ordering a full recount.

The Bush legal team went back to the U.S. Supreme Court, and the justices again agreed to hear the case, stopping the recount ordered by the Florida Supreme Court while the case proceeded. After oral arguments and a weekend of deliberations, the Court, by a 5-4 vote that broke along ideological grounds (the five most conservative justices supported the Bush side, and the four most liberal justices supported Gore), decided that it was too late for a full recount and that there were no objective standards for such a recount. In effect, by putting an end to the wrangling, the Supreme Court chose George W. Bush as president-elect. Days later, Gore conceded once and for all, saying he disagreed with the decision but would respect the process.

Figure 1.1   Might Chief Justice Rehnquist have said something to George W. Bush? Cartoon by Laura Gunther.

Some argue that the justices were "forced" into accepting the case by the judicial activism of the Florida Supreme Court. The unsigned opinion for the majority concluded with a recognition that the Court was on dangerous turf:

> None are more conscious of the vital limits on judicial authority than are the members of this Court, and none stand in more admiration of the Constitution's design to leave the selection of the President to the people, through their legislatures, and to the political sphere. When contending parties invoke the process of the courts, however, it becomes our unsought responsibility to resolve the federal and constitutional issues the judicial system has been forced to confront.

What gave the U.S. Supreme Court the authority to intervene in the dispute? Should the Court have stayed out of the controversy? The constitutional provisions covering such situations are vague, as are the statutory provisions dealing with voting. Did the justices use their own views and their own preferences, rather than legal factors such as precedent, statutory authority, or relevant constitutional provisions? In her dissent, Justice Ruth Bader Ginsburg charged that the five justices who were willing to interfere with the judgment of a state court had long traditions of giving state governments and courts a great deal of discretion and control over their jurisdictions.[1] If this was a question of state law, shouldn't the Florida courts, and not a federal court, make the decision?

The divisions on the Court were sharp and visible to the public. Justice Stephen Breyer claimed, "There is no justification for the majority's remedy, which is simply to reverse the lower court and halt the recount entirely." He concluded, "I fear that in order to bring this agonizingly long election process to a definitive conclusion, we have not adequately attended to that necessary 'check upon our exercise of power,' 'our own sense of self-restraint.'"

Many analysts were critical of the Supreme Court for getting involved in an issue that was outside its business. The nine unelected justices had decided the election was over by the narrowest of margins, reflecting the divisions in the public. By carrying Florida, Bush had won the electoral vote. However, some charged that because the Supreme Court had not allowed the state to finish its recount, he was not the actual winner in Florida. In addition, Gore had won the national popular vote. Many argued that the Court had overstepped its authority. They claimed it had put its institutional reputation and *legitimacy* on the line. Justice John Paul Stevens joined the chorus of criticism in his dissent: "Time will one day heal the wound to that confidence that will be inflicted by today's decision. One thing, however, is certain. Although we may never know with complete certainty the identity of the winner of this year's presidential election, the identity of the loser is perfectly clear. It is the nation's confidence in the judge as an impartial guardian of the rule of law." Would this decision become a self-inflicted wound that permanently harms the Supreme Court?

This book cannot conclusively answer these questions, but it can provide a context for addressing such questions and for considering one of the classic dilemmas of American politics: What is the appropriate role of the U.S. Supreme Court? The facts that spawned *Bush v. Gore* are not likely to recur anytime soon. But the Supreme Court will continue to make important decisions and become embroiled in controversies. Questions will continue to arise: Should the Supreme Court be an active policymaker like Congress and the president? What factors are legitimate for justices to consider when making a decision? There is a great deal of controversy over the appropriate role of the Supreme Court. I will define the scope of that controversy and the terms *legitimacy, judicial activism,* and *judicial restraint* as a prelude to a discussion of this dilemma of American politics.

Note

1. The majority argued that it needed to protect the state legislature's authority from the state courts.

1

The Supreme Court: Law or Politics?

．．．

T HE IMAGES ARE BURNED into the American psyche, shown on the evening news and emblazoned on the front page of newspapers: Angry white parents on school grounds and at school board meetings protest the busing of their children to achieve racial balance; right-to-life protesters, often brandishing pictures of a partially formed fetus, picket a clinic and loudly urge women to reconsider the decision to abort their pregnancies; a male denounces a company's decision to promote a woman he considers less qualified or less experienced to the position he sought. Abortion, busing, and affirmative action are three of the most controversial issues in American society, and they share some important features. First, the Constitution is silent about each of these issues. Second, major landmark decisions made by the U.S. Supreme Court virtually define public policy in these issue areas, which is noteworthy, in part, because the nine justices of the Supreme Court, who are unelected, have become policymakers—typically thought to be the domain of elected officials. In addition, justices are appointed for life, and once appointed they are largely beyond the reach of the public, Congress, and the president.

In *The Federalist Papers*, Alexander Hamilton referred to the judiciary as "the least dangerous branch of government." For many years, or according to the judicial myth (the view that courts are neutral arbiters who do not make the law but find the law), courts and judges were not viewed as policymakers. Yet as early as the nineteenth century, Alexis de Tocqueville, a foreign observer of American politics, wrote, "There is hardly a political question in the United States which does not sooner or later turn into a judicial one." In the 1930s and again since the 1950s, when people have criticized the Supreme Court, it has not been because it was too weak or unwilling to exercise its authority. Rather, it has been because the Supreme Court was seen as an "imperial judiciary" by those who believe that all courts to a degree, but especially the Supreme Court, have become a supreme power by abusing their authority. How are these apparently contradictory notions reconciled? Today, concern for the policymaking activities of courts is the subject of political debate and scholarly attention. These concerns were brought into sharp focus in *Bush v. Gore*.

One of the classical dilemmas in American politics and the subject of this book is, What *is* the appropriate role for the U.S. Supreme Court? The question comes down to the policymaking activity of the Court: Should the Court, because its members are unelected or because it deals with questions of a legal nature, be a policymaker? The public has long been conditioned to believe that the law and legal questions require disinterested decisions. The statue of Thebes, blindfolded and holding the scales of justice, is the image of law in the United States. It is often noted that the Court "lacks the sword and the purse," meaning it cannot enforce its own decisions. Should the Court, despite these weaknesses, be a coequal branch of government charged with making public policy?

In establishing the blueprint for our form of government, the framers of the Constitution were guided by historical precedent and political theory. Borrowing liberally from Montesquieu and Locke, they sought to establish a limited government, controlled by separating legislative, executive, and judicial powers and giving each branch some authority to check the other branches. The constitutional notion of separation of powers suggests that Congress makes the laws, the president executes them, and the Supreme Court interprets them. Theoretically, this configuration divides the policy process into neat stages: Public officials and external actors approach the government in the agenda stage, Congress formulates and adopts a solution, and the president and the bureaucracy implement the program. The Supreme Court may be asked to interpret provisions or assess their constitutionality. In reality, these stages blur; American politics is not so neat.

In considering the controversy over the appropriate role of the Court, this book examines a number of dimensions of the dilemma. The current debate was fueled by the controversial decision to end the recount in Florida. But the nature of the debate has changed over time. An argument is considered normative if it prescribes what ought to be. Normative propositions are value judgments that can be neither proved nor disproved. An empirical argument, on the other hand, is based on what is. Empirical propositions are based on evidence. In the beginning, broad normative notions of democratic theory and institutional concerns dominated arguments about the appropriate role for the Court. Based on the fact that the justices are not elected, and given the perceived constraints on judicial power, analysts have argued on normative grounds that the Court should not make public policy. More recently, an empirical dimension regarding the capacity of the Court to make effective policy has been added to the normative concerns.

This is not a book that systematically examines all aspects of the Supreme Court; there are already a number of excellent treatments available (Baum 2001 and O'Brien 2000 are two of the most popular). Rather, this is an examination of one of the most important and enduring issues in American politics: the debate over the appropriate role of the Supreme Court in American politics.

Defining the Dilemma

The dilemma of the appropriate role of the Court is usually framed in terms of judicial restraint and judicial activism. I define these in broad terms to reflect a number of elements of decisionmaking.

Judicial restraint is defined as the Court's willingness to confine the use and extent of its power. Judicial restraint follows the notion that because justices are unelected and the Supreme Court is relatively weak, the Court should operate at the margins and avoid making public policy. Restraint normally means that the justices will faithfully apply precedents (previous decisions of the Court in similar cases) and defer to the elected branches. The normative view of courts typically holds that the exercise of restraint by judges is considered the ideal and appropriate use of judicial power. Institutionally, judicial restraint means that the Supreme Court should interpret the law, rather than make the law. Congress and the president should make public policy, rather than the Court. As a consequence, the Court should make narrow decisions. The Court, then, is a relatively weak branch of government that has to rely on its institutional legitimacy (its authority) to preserve its power (Baum 2001, 5–6).

Judicial activism, on the other hand, indicates the Court's willingness to make significant changes in public policy. Activism occurs when the justices go beyond the Court's limitations and "make" law, rather than merely interpret it. For individual justices, activism and restraint are often considered functions of the extent to which their own political beliefs and values influence their decisions (Wolfe 1997, 1). Institutionally, judicial activism means that the Supreme Court is willing to exercise its power to the fullest, make sweeping public policy, and ignore existing precedents and the elected branches. Activism is frequently criticized as beyond the scope of judicial power, and judicial activism has been used as a code word to express disapproval with a decision, a justice, or the Court (Justice 1997b, 302). Critics charge that the Court risks its legitimacy when it is too activist.

In theory, there are differences in how broadly justices decide cases. Proponents of judicial restraint would concentrate on interpreting precedents, statutes, and constitutional provisions according to some defined principles and would defer to the elected branches and existing precedents. Presumably a Supreme Court decision based on legal factors would have a great deal of legitimacy attached to it.

Judicial activism, on the other hand, sees justices as aggressive policymakers who use the vagueness of statutory and constitutional provisions as an opportunity to pursue their policy goals (using so-called extralegal factors). Critics charge that justices often "legislate" from the bench and that courts have become "super-legislatures," making the law rather than finding it. Further, critics claim, the

Court is making increasingly broader decisions that go far beyond the two parties in the case. Expansive lawmaking or policymaking by unelected justices exposes the Court to criticism that could undermine its legitimacy. But I'm getting a little ahead of the story. I have some details to fill in first.

It is important to note that though many people equate judicial activism with liberalism and restraint with being conservative, these connections are not necessarily accurate. An activist Court could be liberal or conservative, depending on its policy goals. Similarly, a liberal Court could exhibit restraint by following precedent or deferring to the elected branches, as could a conservative Court.

I have been using the term *legitimacy.* Concern for the legitimacy of the Supreme Court is an important component of the dilemma. If the Court oversteps its boundaries, it risks losing its legitimacy. Legitimacy can be defined in a number of ways. Most simply, it refers to the authority of the institution (in this case, the Supreme Court). Legitimacy is a characteristic of a political institution whereby it has both a legal and a perceived right to make binding decisions. Legitimacy is granted to an institution by the public when it conforms to its established procedures (Shafritz 1992, 334). Because legitimacy means having the approval of others, the condition of being believable is crucial to the Court's ability to fulfill its perceived roles (Lawson 1993, 41). In short, political legitimacy means having widespread approval for the way one exercises political power.

Normative ideals suggest that exercising restraint, using the proper bases for decisions, and making narrow decisions would grant the Court greater legitimacy than activism, which uses extralegal factors and makes broader policy decisions. If the answer was that easy, though, there would be no need for the remainder of this book. There are a number of dimensions to the dilemma concerning the appropriate role of the Court and its policymaking.

Making Public Policy: Does the Supreme Court Take Part?

When Americans think of public policy, they normally consider Congress and the president as the sources. Democratic theory considers these to be the appropriate locations for policymaking. After all, if the public is unhappy with the policies that emerge from the White House or the Capitol, voters can throw the scoundrels out of office in the next national election. When the justices announce a decision such as *Roe v. Wade* (1973) that may offend as many people as it pleases, the public seems helpless. There is no November election to remove Chief Justice William Rehnquist, who opposes the constitutional right to reproductive freedom, or Justice John Paul Stevens, who supports a woman's right to choose.

Despite the activities of the Supreme Court in areas such as school desegregation, abortion, and freedom of expression, there has been a long-term reluctance to view the Court and the justices as active policymakers. Part of this reluctance stems from the venerable judicial myth that judges do not make the law, but they find the law in the Constitution and existing precedents and apply it. Remnants of that belief have filtered into the widely held normative view that unelected judges should not make policy because they are unfettered by those devices that define representative and democratic governance. Vigorous academic debates about the proper role of the Court (Bickel 1975; Bork 1990; McDowell 1982), the relative merits of judicial activism (Perry 1982; Tribe 1985; Miller 1982b) and judicial restraint (Bickel 1975; Berger 1977; Wolfe 1997), the appropriate standards for judicial review (Choper 1980; Wechsler 1959), and acceptable ways of interpreting the Constitution (Ducat 1978; Goldstein 1991) have inspired debate among public officials (Meese 1985; Brennan 1986; 1987). More recently, arguments opposing judicial policymaking have been substantiated by studies suggesting that the courts lack the capacity to make public policy (Horowitz 1977), that the judiciary is constrained in its abilities, and that analysts have exaggerated the impact of the courts on public policy and society (Rosenberg 1991).

If the justices of the Supreme Court are not policymakers, then there is no reason for concern. After listening to the justices' public comments at their confirmation hearings, citizens might well believe that justices do not make public policy. Law and politics are often thought of as comprising different ends of a hypothetical continuum. Law is conceived of as neutral and above politics. The legal realm is typically distinguished from public policymaking, and courts are supposedly neutral arbiters.

Despite the public protests and statements to the contrary by virtually every nominee to the Supreme Court, particularly when addressing the Senate Judiciary Committee,[1] justices are in an institutional position to make public policy and their decisions contribute to the authoritative allocation of values that emanate from the Supreme Court. Furthermore, their behavior once they reach the Court belies their statements that they come with no agenda and no preconceived notions about the issues that reach them as cases. In most issue domains, research shows that justices exhibit consistency in their decisionmaking that reflects their long-held values and attitudes (Segal and Spaeth 1993).

The Supreme Court is a legal institution, to be sure. As Lawrence Baum (2001, 3) notes, the Court makes decisions "within the framework of the law." That does not mean that it is not also a political institution. The Court hears arguments on some of the most controversial issues of the day. The perceived distinctions between the legal and political represent a false dichotomy. As Oliver Wendell Holmes remarked, "Every important principle which is developed by litigation is, in fact and at bottom, the result of more or less definitely understood views of public policy" (Wahlbeck 1997, 779). To determine whether justices make public policy requires first defining the concept.

Public policy has been defined in a number of ways to describe processes by which issues are considered or ignored (Baumgartner and Jones 1993; Kingdon 1995, 3); the work of governmental institutions; and various substantive outcomes, such as "energy policy" or "economic policy" (Dunn 1981, 46–47; Smith 1993). Policy constitutes the responses and nonresponses to perceived problems. Policy has been defined as the establishment and application of "authoritative rules by which government institutions seek to influence the operation of government and to shape society as a whole" (Baum 2001, 4).

As the third and "least dangerous branch" (*The Federalist* 78), the judiciary was charged with interpreting the Constitution and statutes. Presumably, this responsibility could be discharged by applying past precedents without making public policy; thus, unelected judges could avoid substituting their preferences for those of elected officials. Indeed, justices sometimes compare themselves with the referees or umpires at a sporting event: They do not make the rules of the game; they merely apply them. There is an increasing recognition, however grudging, that all courts, regardless of their station in the federal or state judicial system, are policymakers, whatever the definition ascribed to policy. Indeed, the baseball umpire with the wide strike zone, or the proverbial Russian judge at an international gymnastics competition, affects the eventual outcome of the contest. There remains controversy over the proper role of the judicial branch and the extent to which courts should make policy, but it is evident that judges are important policymakers.

Two quotes by justices who served together on the Supreme Court reflect the different notions of whether judges make policy. A classic quotation by Justice Owen Roberts sums up the contention that justices do not make policy:

> It is sometimes said that the court assumes a power to overrule or control the action of the people's representatives. This is a misconception. The Constitution is the supreme law of the land ordained and established by the people. . . . When an act of Congress is appropriately challenged in the courts as not conforming to the constitutional mandate the judicial branch of the Government has only one duty—to lay the article of the Constitution which is invoked beside the statute which is challenged and to decide whether the latter squares with the former. (*United States v. Butler* 297 US 1 [1935])

Contrast that with a statement by Chief Justice Charles Evan Hughes: "We live under a Constitution, but the Constitution is what judges say it is" (Wolfe 1997, 30).

These competing conceptions remain in force today. When presidents are considering nominating a prospective justice to the Supreme Court, they invariably say that they want someone who will interpret the law rather than make it. They want someone who will apply legal principles rather than make policy from the bench. A senator who rises in the chamber to state an objection or support for the nominee uses the same phrases. In essence, that senator wants someone who will not legislate from the Court and who will leave lawmaking to the branches that the Constitution constructed for that purpose. Certainly, elected officials are smart enough to know that when the justices issue a decision, it has the force of law and changes the nature of the relationship between the state and the individual or between two individuals. What they are seeking is a minimal amount of aggressive lawmaking by the unelected justice, but they are also seeking to appoint and confirm a justice who will reflect their views.

It is a truism that American courts make law; they always have made law, and presumably they always will (Gambitta, May, Foster 1981, 9). Judges in medieval England made law through common law practices. American judges did the same thing. *Common law* refers to laws made by judges that occurred in the absence of any statutory provisions. As legislatures wrote more laws, there was less common law for judges to make.

Lawmaking or policymaking also occurs when judges fill gaps in existing statutes and when they interpret statutes, administrative rules and regulations, executive orders, and previous judicial decisions. Courts make policy when they interpret constitutional provisions or decide whether an action is constitutional. To paraphrase Bishop Hoadley, the person with the authority to interpret the law is truly the lawgiver. In some senses, interpretation equals the power to govern (Miller 1982a, 170).

That is a great deal of authority and power, to be sure. However, courts have not limited themselves to simply striking down laws. They have also issued positive edicts, prescribing governmental behavior, and establishing official state policy. Not only do courts decide individual cases but they construct legal rules and design social remedies, such as busing, that go beyond the individual litigants. Litigation beckons the courts to get involved with the controversial issues of the day (Gambitta, May, and Foster 1981, 11), an involvement that has led many to the conclusion that courts govern America.

It is clear that when the justices unanimously decided that it was illegal to segregate white and black students (*Brown v. Board of Education* [1954]), the Court was making public policy. When a majority of the justices ruled that police must have a warrant to search a home (*Mapp v. Ohio* [1961]) and must read a suspect his rights (*Miranda v. Arizona* [1965]), the Court was making policy. No one seems concerned when the Court chooses to uphold a legislative act or interprets the statute in a manner that seems consistent with the intent of the Congress that passed it. Whether the Court issues a major landmark or a relatively minor decision, the justices choose one party over another. In doing so, the Court allocates some authoritative value, a central component of policymaking. More importantly, the Court's decision sets a precedent or a guide for the lower courts. Even if the decision does not have wide-ranging effects and goes largely unnoticed, it is a substantive choice between two competing principles. It is clear that judicial policymaking is inevitable, but activism is a matter of choice.

The policy that emerges from the Supreme Court has some similarities to the policies issued by the elected branches of government. To be sure, the Court operates under a series of constraints that are unlike those facing the other branches, including the fact that the Court lacks "the sword and the purse." In a broad sense, decisions of the Court—like presidential decrees, administrative regulations, and congressional legislation—carry legitimacy. Supreme Court decisions, however, carry additional weight: They carry the force of the Constitution because many cases involve some interpretation of that document's provisions.

There is also a symbolic aura that is ascribed to the Court, and thus its decisions, similar to that attached to the presidency but different in nature. The Supreme Court is the most respected branch and the least known by the public. The Court has long held a "diffuse support" that is separate from individual decisions and separable from the individual justices, whose names and views are a mystery to the vast majority of the population (Murphy and Tanenhaus 1968; Goldman and Jahnige 1985, 108–117).[2] The cult of the Court—tied inexorably to notions of justice, the symbolism of the black robes, and the marble palace—is responsible in part for this diffuse support (Brigham 1987, 63).

Policies emerging from the Court are also similar to policies that emanate from other branches of government in that they are long-term and made up of a series of pronouncements over time. Supreme Court policy is found in judicial doctrine, which in turn is found in the Court's decisions in the individual areas of law. The interpretations of constitutional provisions and the definition of rights and liberties result from the resolution of individual questions that arise in the variety of cases that reach the Court.

By virtue of its position at the apex of the judicial system, the Supreme Court has to fulfill some obligations. Perhaps most importantly, the Court is charged with the responsibility of introducing stability into the law to guide the lower courts and to set standards that inform citizens of their rights and the limitations on their behavior. The Court's ability to achieve this and appear to be above politics can enhance its diffuse support and, in turn, its legitimacy. Too many controversial decisions, on the other hand, can erode support and undermine the Court's legitimacy.

Symbolically, the nine robed individuals, insulated from the reach of public opinion and accountability, appear to represent a council of elders who decide fundamental questions defining societal relationships. In effect, justices have the authority to "amend" and "rewrite" the Constitution by their interpretation in individual cases. Because the Constitution is the foundation of this form of government, the Court has considerable status, conferring on its justices the title of political theorists (Lowi 1968). Procedurally, this role may result from the fact that the Court offers extensive written justifications for its institutional decisions. Furthermore, complementary and competing views may also find their way into print in concurring and dissenting opinions. The written opinions of the justices represent their individual and collective judgments about the meaning of constitutional provisions and the state of social, political, and economic relationships. The long-term construction of doctrine suggests that the political theory emerging from the Court is cumulative and evolutionary in scope. Before considering the different exercises of judicial power and their relation to the dilemma, I will briefly examine the Supreme Court as an institution.

The Supreme Court

The U.S. Supreme Court is a unique institution. It has far more power than the high courts of most other nations. The Supreme Court differs from most of its international counterparts in its ability to review the work of other branches of government; as a result, the Court plays a more fundamental role in making public policy. Some of the newer nations, or those that have revised their constitutions, have created courts in the image of the U.S. Supreme Court. The Court's extensive power raises an inevitable question of how the Supreme Court should be characterized: Is it the least dangerous branch of government, or is it part of an imperial judiciary?

The Supreme Court is a peculiar institution for a democracy, given that its members are not elected and serve for life. The justices operate in relative secrecy and low visibility. For the most part, the public does not understand how the Supreme Court works or know the justices' names, and the Court seems to like it that way. It is also a peculiar institution for a policymaker. The Supreme Court is not a self-starter: The justices must wait for petitions to be brought before them. If members of Congress perceive a problem and desire to do something about it, they can simply draft a bill and put it in the hopper. If the president wishes to attack a certain problem, he can suggest a program to Congress in his State of the Union address or formulate an executive order. If justices of the Supreme Court wish to declare an act of Congress unconstitutional or do something about gay or lesbian rights, they cannot simply decide those issues. Rather, they have to wait for an appropriate case that raises the issues about which they are concerned. This can limit the ability of the Court to be systematic in addressing public policy issues.

The Supreme Court is an active participant in making policy. For some issues the Court is a secondary policymaker, supplementing the work of the elected branches. In other areas, most notably the domain of individual liberties, the Court has been the central policymaker, and its pronouncements dominate those areas of law. Through its decisions, the Supreme Court interprets the Constitution and various statutes and thereby assists in the construction of policy. The Supreme Court has responsibility for applying constitutional provisions to specific circumstances.

Issues of public policy are brought to the judiciary in the form of legal questions posed in the various cases. These questions require some interpretation of legislation, administrative regulations, past judicial precedents, or provisions of the Constitution. In selecting certain cases for review, in deciding the scope of that review, and in the ultimate decisions on the merits, the Supreme Court makes important choices and allocates important resources. In short, the Court makes public policy. At the same time, the decisions contribute to the construction of doctrine. The justices have a desire to impose consistency on doctrine, thus trying to abide by precedent.

The Supreme Court is the one national governmental institution that has to justify its decisions and policy choices in writing. Whereas a law of Congress or an executive order lays out a policy, a Court decision explains the policy position and provides extensive justification for the decision. That decision may be based on constitutional grounds. The decision will also be nested within the context of a series of precedents from similar cases. The need to justify their decisions provides the justices with the opportunity to continue the construction of an evolving democratic theory.

When a vacancy occurs on the Supreme Court, the president gets to exercise a powerful constitutional prerogative, with the advice and consent of the Senate. If the Supreme Court were not a policymaker, it would not matter who a president selected to the bench, as long as the nominee was eminently qualified. Reality suggests otherwise. As noted earlier in this chapter, presidents often argue that they seek a justice who will not make the law, but, rather, will interpret it. They often claim to seek someone who will exercise judicial restraint. But when a president nominates an individual to the high court, he seeks to find a justice who will reflect his views. Presidents normally select well-respected legal scholars who also happen to reflect a certain demographic profile. Presidents have not been above using a Supreme Court nomination to shore up electoral support, pay off a campaign debt, or advance a crony's career. Since the Nixon administration, presidents have been more attentive to the policy potential of nominations and less likely to use a vacancy for demographic purposes, such as religion or region (Abraham 1999).[3]

The selection of a new justice for the Supreme Court is one of the most important responsibilities of the presidency. Long after presidents have left office, their nominees can affect the course of American public policy. Questions exist as to the effects of the so-called Reagan Revolution. Most analysts maintain that President Ronald Reagan failed to secure his economic and social policies. No one can dispute that the Reagan Court—begun by Richard Nixon, augmented by a number of Reagan appointees, and completed by the first George Bush—has had and will continue to have an important role in shaping relations among the three branches, the national and subnational governments, and between individuals and the state.

To put it in perspective, when William Douglas left the Court in 1975, that officially ended President Franklin D. Roosevelt's direct impact on the Supreme Court. Indirectly, FDR's influence has continued as the remaining justices and new members of the Court address the precedents and constitutional interpretations left by Douglas and his brethren over the previous decades. Similarly, long after Rehnquist and Scalia leave the Court, their legacy will be bequeathed to those who ascend the bench. Given normal actuarial expectations, the president who will get the opportunity to select Clarence Thomas's replacement may currently be a student in high school.

The process by which the Supreme Court makes its decisions gives the justices a number of opportunities to make policy. At the initial stage, the justices have more than 7,000 petitions on their docket to consider. Annually, they accept 100–150 of these petitions. In taking certain cases and refusing others, the Court makes policy. By declining a petition, the Supreme Court lets the lower court decision stand and refuses access to the issue in that case. For many years, the Court refused to consider questions involving gay and lesbian rights, a policy of neglect, as public policy is defined as decisions and nondecisions.

It is relatively easy to see how the Supreme Court makes policy when it accepts a case. In announcing a decision, the justices choose one litigant over the other. The Court's decision is a written justification of the final result. That decision, called the opinion of the Court, is a precedent that is binding on lower courts and on the Supreme Court in similar future cases. In a sense, the Court's decision is like a congressional statute in that it is the law of the land.

The Court makes policy when it upholds a precedent, when it faithfully inter-prets a statute or a constitutional provision, and when it declares an act of Con-gress constitutional. No one seems too bothered by any of those because they rep-resent examples of judicial restraint. The Court also makes policy when it overturns a precedent, expands or contracts statutory provisions, "rewrites" a pro-vision of the Constitution, or declares an act of Congress unconstitutional. Each of those examples tends to be associated with judicial activism and opens the Court to controversy.

The handiwork of the framers of the Constitution has had unintended conse-quences. Justices were insulated so they could be disinterested and above the winds of political change. The Supreme Court was designed to embody the nor-mative ideal of a government of laws, not of men and women. If the justices use their insulation to make the law rather than find it, to substitute their judgment for that of the elected officials, and to rewrite the Constitution, the charter of our government, then the questions that motivate this book become very important.

Unraveling the Dilemma

How exactly does the Court make policy? In one sense, every decision the justices make allocates some value to one of the parties in the case. No matter how in-significant the case, the choice of one litigant over another represents a policy choice. However, policy can take many forms. The Court's decision can be narrow and confined to the two parties in the case or the decision can be sweeping and designed to create large-scale changes. To the extent that the Court narrows its de-cisions, it finds itself closer to the judicial restraint end of the spectrum. However, if the Court expands its decision, it is opting for judicial activism.

When analysts who study the Supreme Court define activism and restraint, they are normally referring to judicial review—the power of the Court to declare an act of Congress or of the president unconstitutional—and how willing the Court was to use it. In truth, the Court seldom exercises judicial review. There are other ways the Court can make policy that mandate expanding the definitions of activism and restraint. Expanding the definitions incorporates precedent. How closely the Court adheres to precedent is a measure of activism and restraint.

I want to extend the definitions a little further to include active policymaking by the Court. When the Court makes sweeping decisions and constructs broad remedies for social ills, it is actively making policy. Christopher Wolfe considers these "modern" variants of judicial activism. Modern judicial activism and re-straint can be defined in terms of the relation of a decision to the Constitution or the manner in which the justices exercise their power. Wolfe (1997, 30, 33) argues that modern judicial activism is defined as the power to revise the Constitution and frees "the justices from ties to the Constitution." Thus, justices can change the meaning of the Constitution by their interpretation of its provisions. Analysts define activism as the willingness of judges to "legislate" from the bench. Throughout the book, then, the term *judicial activism* is used to refer both to the narrow traditional meaning and the expanded notion of active policymaking by the Court.

Courts make policy, but how much and by what standards encapsulate the dilemma. Supreme Court policymaking takes a variety of different forms. Four separate situations seem to define the brand of active judicial policymaking that is at the heart of the dilemma. There are two components that yield the four situations: traditional versus modern activism and internal versus external constraints on the Court. Table 1.1 shows that traditional concerns with activism and restraint involve judicial review and precedent. Modern activism reflects the expansion of the Court's decisions and the construction of broad remedies. The other component determines whether the justices are reviewing their past interpretations or whether the Court is reviewing the work of external actors, such as Congress and the president, in exerting judicial activism.

The Court faces more constraints when external actors are involved than when its decision is internal. The decision to declare an act of Congress unconstitutional means that the Court is rejecting a policy that passed both houses and was signed by the president. The use of judicial review is a traditional exercise of activism. In statutory interpretation, a decision that expands or contracts congressional provisions so as to change the meaning of a statute passed by elected officials also involves external actors, but represents the modern definition of activist policymaking. Or, in a traditional exercise of activism that is internal to the institution, the Court can reverse existing precedent. As an example of modern activism that is internally derived, the Court can stretch or contract its interpretation of constitutional provisions to include the creation of new rights or the destruction of old ones.

Each of these situations raises questions about the appropriate role of the Supreme Court. Table 1.2 shows what constitutes restraint and activism in each of the four categories. In the first two instances, unelected judges are substituting their collective judgment for the elected branches. The second instance, in particular, is frequently interpreted as the Court substituting its judgment for Congress. In the last two situations, because internal decisionmaking is dominant, there is a sense that changes in the composition of the Court have been the sole reason for changes in the law. In the third circumstance, the Court takes an established

TABLE 1.1   The Components of Judicial Activism and Restraint

Notions of Activism and Restraint	Decisional Constraints	
	Internal	External
Traditional	Precedent	Judicial review
Modern	Constitutional interpretation	Statutory interpretation

Source: Richard Pacelle.

TABLE 1.2   Manifestations of Judicial Activism and Restraint for Each Activity of Judicial Policymaking

Activity	Judicial Role	
	Restraint	Activism
Statutory interpretation	Fill gaps consistent with legislative intent	Rewrite/expand/contract statutory provisions
Judicial review	Uphold legislation defer to elected branches	Overturn legislation
Precedent	Adhere/defer to existing precedent	Overturn/distinguish existing precedent
Constitutional interpretation	Narrow/consistent with broad neutral principles Judicial interpretation	Broad interpretation Rewrite provisions Judicial legislation

Source: Richard Pacelle.

precedent, which has created predictability in the law and changes it. In the fourth category, the Court is open to the charge that the Constitution can be changed with the times and is a mere reflection of the current majority of justices. In these instances, the justices may go beyond the legal factors that are supposed to govern decisionmaking. Judicial restraint is the avoidance of these four situations.

There is an individual-level dimension to the dilemma as well. Activist justices may be less willing to tie their decision to legal factors and instead rely solely on their values and preferences. In other words, the justices could decide cases based on their conception of what the end result should be. Advocates of restraint would base their decisions on legal factors: the Constitution, some set of shared accepted values, or existing precedents. They would confine their interpretations of statutes to filling in the margins, rather than changing the scope of the legislation. The individual level dimension will be examined in Chapter 6. First, these four controversial exercises of judicial power need to be considered more closely.

Statutory Construction: Changing the Meaning

Statutory interpretation provides the opportunity for the Court to change the handiwork of Congress. Does the Court seek to fill in the gaps consistent with congressional designs or does it try to expand its own views? The statute to be construed had to pass a series of political barriers to be enacted. It must survive committees in both houses of Congress, votes on the floors of both houses, and often a conference committee where members of Congress hammer out differences between the versions that passed each chamber. Then, in most instances, it needs the signature of the president or, if vetoed, must be passed again by an extraordinary majority. In American politics, however, the game is still not over. Unelected bureaucrats have to formulate rules and regulations to implement the new law. Groups and individuals unhappy with the new law or its implementation may go to the courts to try to have the law interpreted more broadly or narrowly. Advocates of judicial restraint would decline this opportunity, opting to try to discover and follow the intent of Congress in passing the law. If the Supreme Court contracts the law, it is, in a sense, ignoring the mandate of the elected branches. By the same token, expanding the law may be adding provisions that Congress specifically rejected. Expanding or contracting the law is an act of judicial activism.

There are numerous examples of such occurrences. Congress passed Title IX of the Educational Amendments Act of 1972, which prohibited sex discrimination in educational programs receiving federal funds. In 1983, the Supreme Court adopted a very narrow interpretation of Title IX in the *Grove City College v. Bell* decision. Title IX imposed an obligation to ensure that federal assistance not be granted to recipients who engage in unlawful gender discrimination. Grove City College itself received no funds, but its students received federal financial aid. The specific question in the case was whether the receipt of federal money by one program (the financial aid program) of the college subjected the entire institution to Title IX.

A bipartisan group of forty-nine members of Congress filed a brief in the case arguing that Congress had intended that the institution would lose all federal funding if there was any discrimination in the college. *Grove City* was important because the Court ignored congressional intent and narrowed the interpretation of Title IX. The Court ruled that providing federal funds to some programs or activities did not permit civil rights regulation of the entire institution (Halpern 1995, 197–198). This would weaken the enforcement of sanctions against gender discrimination (Hoff 1991, 242). The decision limited the scope of Title IX and spilled over to other civil rights enforcement (Lindgren and Taub 1993, 279).

In the wake of *Grove City*, Congress sought to restore teeth to Title IX. For two years, Senate opponents successfully filibustered the Civil Rights Restoration Act, which said if a college receives any federal funds, the entire institution is covered (Cheney 1998, 38). Eventually, the act passed, but was vetoed by President Reagan, who supported the narrow position of the Court. Both houses of Congress were able to muster the votes to override the president's veto and overrule *Grove City*, restoring the intended force of Title IX.

There were also Supreme Court decisions that widely extended the reach of statutes. In passing the monumental Civil Rights Act of 1964, Congress took pains to note that this law would not endorse notions of affirmative action. Members of Congress had dismissed allegations that the Civil Rights Act would require "hiring, firing, or promotion of employees in order to meet a racial 'quota' or achieve a certain racial balance" (Graham 1990, 109–113). Over time, the Supreme Court began to lengthen the reach of the Civil Rights Act, so that it would eventually encompass and support affirmative action as a remedy for the effects of past discrimination. This process began in earnest in 1971, so that less than a decade after passage of the Civil Rights Act, the Court had changed the interpretation of many of its provisions. An activist Court created a statutory right that a majority of Congress had specifically rejected when the law was passed.

Judicial Review

In either of the previous cases of statutory interpretation, if Congress is unhappy with the Court's interpretation, it can overturn the decision as it did with the Civil Rights Restoration Act and with a number of civil rights and voting rights measures in the 1980s. But what happens if the Supreme Court decides an act of Congress is unconstitutional? That is much more difficult to overturn. A simple act of Congress is not enough. The only way to negate a Supreme Court decision that declares an act of Congress unconstitutional is to propose and ratify an amendment to the Constitution. Because that takes the votes of extraordinary majorities—two-thirds of both houses of Congress and three-quarters of the states—the prospects for success are very limited indeed.[4]

When the Supreme Court upholds a law, it legitimizes that law and transfers its legitimacy to the other branches (Dahl 1957). By contrast, when it overturns an act of Congress or the president, it may de-legitimize those branches to a degree. The Court's decision suggests that there is a fatal flaw in the statute that was overturned. Judicial activists would be willing to use the power of judicial review to strike offending legislation. They would act, confident in the knowledge that their decision would not be overturned. Advocates of restraint, on the other hand, would be loath to declare acts of Congress unconstitutional.

In 1989, the Supreme Court ruled that the act of burning the American flag was constitutionally protected freedom of expression. As a result, Congress almost immediately passed the Flag Protection Act. Congress can sometimes get around constitutional decisions by writing a statute that tries to meet the Court's objections to the original statute. In passing the act, Congress was responding to overwhelming public opinion that favored protection of the flag. In 1990, however, the Court declared the act unconstitutional, saying, in effect, that the only way to overturn the decision was to pass an amendment to the Constitution that would prohibit the burning of this national symbol. A number of attempts by Congress have failed to achieve the necessary majorities (Cheney 1998, 45–48).

Perhaps the most serious problems for the Court arise when a new political party sweeps into power. Analysts refer to this periodic political phenomenon as a partisan realignment. Every generation or so, a crisis arises, and one party, usually the party out of power at the time, is perceived as being better able to handle the crisis. Voters then turn against the majority party and support the new party, which goes on to govern for the next generation (Sundquist 1983). For example, with the onset of the Great Depression, the perception that the Republicans under President Herbert Hoover were either unequipped or unwilling to do anything to pull the nation out of the economic cataclysm led voters to switch party allegiance, elect Franklin Roosevelt to the White House, and provide him with a Democratic majority in both houses of Congress. Roosevelt, with the help of Congress, launched an ambitious program, known as the New Deal, to help pull the country out of the Depression.

These new policies had to face judicial scrutiny. The problem for the Roosevelt administration and the Democratic Congress was that most of the justices had been appointed by Republican presidents and shared the views of Hoover and others that government programs to regulate and stimulate the economy were violations of the Constitution. Thus, "the nine old men," as they were derisively called, found large portions of the New Deal unconstitutional. Despite the overwhelming repudiation of the Republican Party by the voters, the GOP held majority control of one branch of government: the Court. The justices were able to thwart the will of the elected branches of government and, presumably, the people.

Eventually, after an enduring realignment, the new majority party will remain in power long enough to fill vacancies on the Court with justices sympathetic to its programs. There are two problems, though. First, the crisis that spawned the realignment needs immediate attention, and with a potentially hostile Court, that could lead to a constitutional crisis. Second, the passage of time allows the new majority party to change the membership of the Court, suggesting that the interpretation of the Constitution can be changed merely by altering the Court's composition.

There is little controversy when the elected branches pass an act that is obviously unconstitutional and the Supreme Court repudiates that law. More often, the decision to strike down a law is controversial and thrusts the Court into the center of a political battle.

Overturning Precedent

The Court needs to create consistency in its decisions and does so by adhering to precedent. Activism, which is measured by changing precedents, introduces instability and uncertainty into the law. The justices can reverse a precedent that existed for generations, which raises the question of why a standard that a past Court adopted in its interpretation of the Constitution is no longer viable. Judicial activists are not constrained by precedent if their policy goals argue otherwise. Advocates of judicial restraint are likely to opt for consistency in the law and would therefore uphold existing precedents, even if they disagreed with them. They maintain that they adhere to precedents because it is more important that the law is settled than settled correctly. Justice Scalia sees a wrinkle, however, claiming that two wrongs, in effect, can make a right: If the original precedent was created out of wanton judicial activism, then the act of reversing that precedent is judicial restraint.

In 1896, the Supreme Court supported racial segregation in its decision in *Plessy v. Ferguson*. In 1954, in *Brown v. Board of Education*, the Court ruled that the notion of "separate but equal," arising from *Plessy*, was no longer valid for public schools. In the intervening half-century, a social custom that had constitutional backing became unacceptable. Nothing in the body of the Constitution had changed to necessitate that new interpretation. Because *Plessy* had come to be seen as wrongly decided, was this ruling judicial activism or restraint?

Precedents tied to federalism have undergone periodic reevaluation. Federalism defines the boundaries between state and national governmental power. The Marshall Court (1801–1835) took a broad view of the Commerce Clause and national authority, thus circumscribing the powers left to the states. However, some dramatic changes occurred in the wake of the Great Depression. The conservative Court struck down many portions of the New Deal on the grounds that the Commerce Clause did not grant Congress the power to combat the economic troubles. This had the effect of limiting national governmental power. Roosevelt attacked the Court and proposed a law to pack the Court with more justices. In the so-called switch in time that saved nine, the Court changed its mind and began upholding the New Deal. In the course of doing so, the Court began to expand the power of the Commerce Clause and the central government. Thus, the Court, in the face of a threat from external forces, wiped out a series of precedents.

For four decades (1937–1976), the Court consistently supported expansion of the Commerce Clause and national power, culminating in *Wickard v. Filburn* (1941), when the Court ruled that Congress could regulate the amount of wheat a farmer could grow for his own consumption. In the 1990s, though, the Rehnquist Court reevaluated the reach of the national government and the breadth of the Commerce Clause. In effect, the Court has strengthened the hand of state governments at the expense of national government (Epstein and Walker 1998a, 400–401). Analysts can argue over which interpretation is the correct one, but it is clear that the Court has changed its position on federalism and the Commerce Clause a number of times, even though the words of the Constitution never changed. Most of those changes could be attributed to changes in the composition of the Court.

Interpreting and Revising Constitutional Provisions

While many can argue with the interpretation of federalism at a given time, it is clear that the Constitution says something about drawing lines between state and national governments. Contrast that with the authority of the Supreme Court to read something into the Constitution that is just not there. The Court's most extensive power, judicial review, is not mentioned anywhere in the Constitution. Rather, Chief Justice John Marshall created the power in *Marbury v. Madison* (1803). Similarly, the constitutional right to privacy is a judicial creation. In his opinion in *Griswold v. Connecticut* (1965), Justice William Douglas wrote that the shadows and penumbras cast by the First, Third, Fourth, and Fifth Amendments created a right to privacy. This, along with the long-dormant Ninth Amendment (offered as justification by Justice Arthur Goldberg), became the basis for *Roe v. Wade* and reproductive rights. In a related issue, the Court found constitutional support for gender equality in the Fourteenth Amendment, although its provisions were designed to apply to race.

In each of these areas, the Court expanded constitutional provisions. There have been cases of taking provisions of the Constitution and radically altering them in the other direction. In the wake of the Civil War and as part of the Union's reconstruction, the Radical Republicans in Congress passed the Thirteenth,[5] Fourteenth, and Fifteenth Amendments. The Fourteenth was the most important, as it sought to ensure equal rights for the freed slaves in the South. Within a decade, however, the Supreme Court gutted the amendment along with a number of statutes that were passed to enforce the three amendments, taking the protections away from African Americans and giving them instead to businesses and corporations (Schwartz 1993, 157–168).

The controversy often revolves around the notions of strict and loose construction of the Constitution. Strict construction refers to following the language of the Constitution as closely as possible. Proponents of this position do not feel that the language and meaning of the Constitution should change with the times. With justices adhering to the language, their individual discretion and the use of outside factors in decisionmaking would supposedly be limited—reflecting judicial restraint.

Loose construction, on the other hand, allows for a broader interpretation of the language of the Constitution; it is viewed as a living document that can be modified to reflect the times. If justices accept the position that the Constitution can change with the times, then they are using extralegal factors or personal values in their decisionmaking.

When the Supreme Court decides to expand or contract constitutional provisions, it can, in essence, change the very nature of the Constitution. In practical terms, it only takes five of the nine justices to "rewrite" the charter of our government. In pursuing their designs, the justices may create broad remedies based on their reading of the Constitution, as the Court did when it mandated busing to achieve desegregation. Significant changes in the interpretation of the Constitution represent clear examples of judicial activism.

Evaluating the Role of the Supreme Court

To this point, it has been established that the Supreme Court is a policymaker. Can any conclusions be drawn from these anecdotes about the Court? At this point, only one thing can be said for sure: Assessing the appropriate role of the Court is a complicated question. Often, support for or opposition to the Court and its exercise of power is predicated on whether the public likes or hates individual decisions. While many advocate the Court adopt judicial restraint, it is important to note that not all forms of judicial activism are bad. In exercising these powers, the Court may be protecting the rights of certain groups and minorities who might have no other source of protection. In the 1950s and 1960s, the have-nots were often able to use the courts to assert rights and benefits that were denied elsewhere.

The Constitution was written at the end of the eighteenth century and can hardly be expected to keep pace with the remarkable social and technological changes of the past two centuries. The Constitution provided next to no rights for women and enslaved blacks. Thus, it may be beneficial for justices to allow the Constitution to change with the times. By the same token, it may serve justice and the common good to overturn antiquated precedents created under completely different circumstances. No one would argue for abiding by old precedents that denied rights to women or segregated the races.

Should the Court be a central actor in making public policy, or should it act at the margins, filling in the details? Should the Court exercise judicial activism and if so, under what conditions? The answers to these questions are tied to notions of legitimacy. According to Christopher Smith (1997, 290), "The legitimacy issue underlying judicial policy making rests on the appropriateness of the judiciary's actions in formulating and implementing public policies." Legitimacy is a political resource. It is fragile and finite, and the Court must conserve and protect it. If the Court oversteps its boundaries, its decisions will not earn the respect of the public or the other branches of government, and its ultimate resource, its legitimacy, will be threatened. It is often argued that the Court risks its legitimacy if the justices are too aggressive in their policymaking. On the other hand, it may be true that the Court can lose legitimacy by doing too little. Will the *Bush v. Gore* decision—which demonstrated some of the risks the Court assumes—eventually cost the Court some of its legitimacy?

A more systematic manner of evaluating the exercise of judicial activism and assessing the appropriate role of the Supreme Court is to consider the dilemma in its various dimensions. There are at least three dimensions to the dilemma surrounding the appropriate role for the Supreme Court and the controversy over judicial restraint and activism. First, there are notions of democratic theory. There is an argument that unelected judges should not make policy—more specifically, they should not substitute their judgment for that of those who are elected. That is the restraintist view. The judicial activist, on the other hand, would not feel bound by majority sentiment. Second, there are institutional-level considerations. There are real constraints on judicial power that suggest that the Court should work at the margins, rather than put itself into the center of policy controversies. Proponents of judicial restraint would subscribe to that view, while activists would try to exercise judicial power to its fullest. Third, and related to the normative institutional concerns, there is an empirical dimension tied to the perceived capacity of the judicial branch to achieve its goals. If the Court has proven itself to be ineffective at making public policy, then it would be advisable for the

Court to restrict its policymaking activity. Certainly, restraintists would argue that the Court should act at the margins. Activists would be willing to exercise the full extent of the institution's power and not worry about the lack of capacity.

As *Bush v. Gore* demonstrated, it is important to remember that the controversies over these different dimensions are not merely part of some sterile academic debate. In addition to the philosophical considerations, there are real policy consequences to these choices. If the Court makes a deliberate attempt to avoid "making law," there will be significant implications for the nature of public policymaking. The consequences will be very different if the Court exercises judicial activism. There are some issues that Congress has failed to address. If the Court were to close its doors to these issues, then these problems might never be addressed. There are also likely to be differences over who will get access to the Court and who wins and loses. Those differences are unlikely to be neutral.

There are important practical political dimensions to this dilemma as well. During the Warren Court (1953–1969), the justices expanded rights and liberties and presided over a constitutional revolution. The Rehnquist Court (1986–present) has adopted a new dominant theory to govern its decisionmaking, which advocates attention to the intent of the framers of the Constitution and a stricter construction of the document. This theory is complemented by an increased willingness to defer to elected branches over civil liberties and civil rights, thus rejecting the twentieth-century liberalism that has guided Court decisions and policymaking in such cases (Smith 1985; Pacelle 1995). If the Rehnquist Court is successful in implementing its designs, then it may mean a less-active policymaking role for the Court and less access for certain groups.

Conclusion

The mix of legal and political traits puts the Supreme Court in the center of policymaking in the United States, but seems to argue for judicial restraint. The dilemma turns on the question of how extensive the Court's policymaking is and what is the appropriate role for the Court. Traditionally, advocates of restraint have urged the Court to use judicial review sparingly, to adhere to precedent, to avoid rewriting statutes or the Constitution, and to make narrow decisions. Judges and analysts have argued for restraint because they feel that the Court is undemocratic, that it faces serious limitations on its power, and because it lacks the capacity to make policy effectively. Whether those concerns are justified will be considered in most of the remainder of this book.

Chapter 2 will examine historical periods when the dilemma of Supreme Court policymaking was most acute; then I consider how our notions of judicial restraint and activism are influenced by each dimension of the dilemma. Chapter 3 examines democratic theory and the role of an unelected institution. Chapter 4 examines institutional concerns, considering the power of the Court and the constraints facing it. Chapter 5 considers notions of judicial capacity. Chapter 6 moves to the individual level of analysis, examining how individual justices make their decisions. Finally, in Chapter 7, I suggest an appropriate role for the Supreme Court in light of the constraints on the institution and its power.

Notes

1. Although it appears to be disingenuous, all nominees sit in front of the Senate Judiciary Committee and publicly proclaim that they come to the Court with no preformed ideas about the issues before the Court. Justices Sandra Day O'Connor and Antonin Scalia refused to answer most specific questions posed by the Judiciary Committee, remarking that they brought no agenda to the bench with them (Abraham 1999). Robert Bork attempted to answer the questions posed, probably because he had an "extensive paper trail" with controversial positions on a number of issues. Opponents were not convinced, "fearing a death bed conversion" to gain confirmation. As a result, recent nominees have returned to refusing to answer most questions. Justice David Souter was labeled the "stealth nominee" for his obscure background and failure to answer questions (Savage 1992, 372). Justice Clarence Thomas left the most controversial inquiries unanswered. Thomas claimed he had not really thought about or discussed *Roe v. Wade* (Savage 1992, 436). Some have argued that one consequence of the Bork nomination is that presidents will seek nominees without "a paper trail."

2. In surveys, less than 5 percent of respondents can name Justices John Paul Stevens, Stephen Breyer, and David Souter. The best-known members of the Court, Sandra Day O'Connor and Clarence Thomas, whose notoriety is tied to their selection rather than their decisions, are named by less than 20 percent of respondents. At the same time, despite the fact that the Court may act like a political institution, reflecting the preferences of a majority of its members, it remains removed from the maelstrom of politics. *Bush v. Gore* changed the visibility of the Court and the justices, at least in the short term. Public support for the Court declined in the wake of that decision. In the past, such declines have been ephemeral. But with this decision, the Court placed itself closer to the center of politics and with less of a cloak to protect it.

3. There are exceptions, however, such as Clarence Thomas.

4. Only a handful of Supreme Court decisions have been reversed by a constitutional amendment. The Eleventh Amendment, overturning *Chisholm v. Georgia,* protects states against suits by citizens of another state. The Fourteenth Amendment overturned *Dred Scott v. Sandford* by conferring citizenship on all people born or naturalized in the United States. The Sixteenth Amendment overturned *Pollock v. Farmers' Loan and Trust,* legalizing the federal income tax. The Twenty-Sixth Amendment, giving eighteen-year-olds the right to vote, overturned *Oregon v. Mitchell.* There have been thousands of proposed amendments that

have been unsuccessful. Some of these were designed to overturn the decisions banning teacher-led school prayer, ordering reapportionment and busing, and permitting abortion and flag burning.

5. The Thirteenth Amendment, which ended slavery, is another example of expanding a constitutional provision well beyond the original intent. In the 1960s, the Supreme Court used it as authority to prevent housing discrimination.

2

The Historical Dimension of the Dilemma

．．

The Constitution, with its broad consensus of philosophical and political ideas, reflects the enduring values that guided the construction and maintenance of the American republic. It has been up to the Supreme Court to interpret that document, and interpretation has changed over time. Despite the fact that the justices are not elected, the Supreme Court does not operate in a vacuum. Societal forces affect the process by which the courts function. The political context sets the boundaries for the courts and influences the construction of doctrine and the individual decisions that create it. Constitutional law is shaped by a dynamic political process that includes Congress and the president. As a consequence, the Constitution adapts over time, combining changes in society with the enduring principles grounded in the document (Fisher 1988, 13–14).

The story of Supreme Court policymaking reflects the historical development of the nation and the Court and the dilemma of the appropriate role of the judicial branch. As with any governmental institution, the Court has changed with the times. Activism and restraint have waxed and waned over time as conditions and demands have changed. The Court has been a central policymaker during some periods and less active during others. What was acceptable in one time period and in one context may not have been during other times.

This chapter is not meant to provide a systematic history of the Supreme Court. There are a number of excellent studies that serve that purpose (for example, Schwartz 1993; McCloskey 1960). Rather, the chapter illustrates five periods when the Supreme Court was an active, sometimes aggressive, policymaker.

As noted in the first chapter, there are four ways in which justices make decisions that smack of judicial activism or aggressive policymaking. First, in statutory interpretation, a decision that significantly expands or contracts the congressional provisions so as to change the very statute represents aggressive policymaking. Second, the decision to declare an act of Congress unconstitutional means that the Court is rejecting a policy that passed Congress and was signed by the president. Third, the Court can reverse an existing precedent. Finally, the Court can stretch or contract its interpretation of constitutional provisions.

While Courts have wavered between exercising almost total judicial restraint and exercising judicial activism—even testing the limits of the Court's legitimacy and endangering its authority—most often, particular Courts have demonstrated activism in some areas and restraint in others. In exercising restraint and activism, a Court may pursue two or three of the activities that define policymaking and eschew the fourth. For instance, a Court may be active in statutory and constitutional interpretation and reversing existing precedents, while at the same time refusing to declare any acts of Congress unconstitutional.

Some of the expansion of judicial power has come from the Court's own initiative in defining or redefining its institutional power. Some has come from the reluctance of the elected branches to address certain issues and the Court's willingness to step in. At other times, the rise in judicial power is externally generated. Courts have not always solicited additional responsibility; they have often had it thrust upon them. The growth of government and the bureaucracy, as well as the proliferation and increased complexity of statutory law, have led to more regulations and more legal conflicts. That means more work for the courts and more potential for Supreme Court intervention (Gambitta, May, and Foster 1981, 13–25).

The Marshall Court (1801–1835)

The first Supreme Court, from the inception of the Constitution in 1789 to 1801, did little to define the powers of the government or the scope of the Constitution. The early Court, reflecting its lack of authority and an institutional role, exhibited clear restraint and seemed relegated to its station as "the least dangerous branch of government." It would take clear judicial activism to reinvent the Court—a job left to John Marshall.

After the defeat of John Adams in the election of 1800, the Supreme Court had little power or authority. The Constitution was a potentially powerful document, but many of its provisions were uncertain. The government was just beginning to develop, and questions involving its power were making their way to the Court—unresolved questions concerning the Commerce Clause and the line separating the authority of the state and the central government. There were few precedents to consult or overturn, so the chief justice was writing on a basically blank slate.

In this environment, Marshall took over as chief justice, largely through the efforts of Federalists trying to pack the judiciary after its philosophy was repudiated in the election. In a sense, Marshall helped breathe life into Article III of the Constitution, defining judicial powers. He became the force behind the creation of judicial review, which has become the primary power of the courts. Judicial review may be an extensive power, but its only use under Marshall occurred in *Marbury v. Madison,* in which the Court—with no clear constitutional authority—declared part of an act passed by Congress unconstitutional.

After *Marbury*, the Marshall Court began to interpret some of the ambiguous provisions of the Constitution. Judge Ruggero Aldisert (1997, 281) argued that it was "interpretation with a vengeance." As a consequence, the Court increasingly ventured into the policymaking realm. Even if the Marshall Court did not use judicial review to strike down additional congressional legislation, it made a number of important decisions that defined congressional authority by expanding the Commerce Clause, enhancing the power of the central government at the expense of the states, and helping business grow and flourish.

Marshall helped reinterpret Article I on legislative powers as well. In *McCulloch v. Maryland* (1819), Marshall achieved two purposes: legitimizing the necessary and proper clause to expand the power of Congress and upholding the supremacy of the central government. In *Gibbons v. Ogden* (1824), Marshall expanded the interpretation of the Commerce Clause, once again enhancing the power of Congress. In each of these decisions, Marshall's interpretation of constitutional provisions curbed state power in the face of majority sentiment to the contrary.

If Charles Evans Hughes's famous quotation "We live under a Constitution, but the Constitution is what we say it is" was ever true, it was in the early nineteenth century. In *Marbury* and *McCulloch*, Marshall expanded constitutional provisions without citing precedent, relying exclusively on his constitutional vision. The Constitution was what John Marshall said it was. He served as chief justice for thirty-four years and left a major imprint on the document and on the law. His interpretations helped build the fledgling government and provided power that had been absent in the early republic. In significant ways, however, Marshall appeared to depart from the intent of the framers of the Constitution and from majority support, exercising clear judicial activism.

History regards Marshall as a great chief justice and probably more influential than any American president. Yet, he has not been immune from criticism for creating judicial review and emasculating state power. The arguments against the creation of judicial review reflect two dimensions of the dilemma concerning the appropriate role of the Court. Judicial review has been criticized because it is antidemocratic and unnecessarily expands the provisions of the Constitution beyond the intent of the framers (Epstein and Walker 1998a, 53–54). The most notable criticism of the time was based on the argument that judicial review posed a threat to legislative supremacy (Wolfe 1997, 12).

Some analysts have argued that Marshall's decisions, which restructured the government, were not acts of judicial activism, but examples of restraint. Indeed, Marshall did not overturn many precedents, in part because few existed. He expanded statutory and constitutional interpretation and made limited use of judicial review. Christopher Wolfe (1997, 10–14) called Marshall's creation "traditional" or "moderate" judicial review. Marshall's constitutional interpretation could be characterized as judicial restraint because it was rooted in the intent of the framers. Marshall inferred from the document as a whole in constructing his tapestry.

Marshall avoided some of the other trappings of judicial activism. The Court did not lay down general laws because that was the role of the legislature. Justices tended to confine their review to the range of issues that were presented in the particular case. The Court's work was largely negative: The justices rejected state provisions that were unconstitutional, but did not try to prescribe positive activities from the other branches of government. In addition, the Court showed deference to the elected branches and demonstrated respect for separation of powers (Wolfe 1997, 13–16).

The Taney Court (1836–1864)

Because there were few prior decisions to guide the Court, Marshall did not have to overturn many precedents. When his successor wanted to redress the balance between state and federal power, however, he would have to confront existing precedents. Roger Taney followed Marshall and served for almost three decades. Indeed, Marshall and Taney were the only chief justices for more than half a century.

Taney was generally regarded as a judicial restraintist. Despite the different philosophies of the Jacksonian Democrats who appointed him, Taney did not reverse the legacy Marshall had left. The Taney Court did not overturn many precedents (only two), but it did modify doctrine. The Court preserved additional authority for the states, advocating what has come to be known as Dual Federalism, a contrast to the National Supremacy doctrine supported by Marshall (Epstein and Walker 1998a).

History does not treat Taney as favorably as it does Marshall, largely because of one decision: *Dred Scott v. Sandford* (1857). The Taney Court became embroiled in the most divisive political issue of the day—slavery expansion. This monumental case, a prime example of judicial activism, involved a slave who had been taken into a free state. The Court decided that slaves could not be citizens and further ruled that Congress could not prevent the spread of slavery into the territories. The decision overturned the Missouri Compromise, an act designed to keep slavery expansion from destroying the union, and thus became only the second use of judicial review by the Court.

The *Dred Scott* decision did not cause the Civil War, but it probably hastened the hostilities. The decision, which has been referred to as "a monstrous piece of judicial effrontery," was considered a "self-inflicted wound" (Newmyer 1968, 139), which means the Court moved so far beyond the boundaries constructed by public opinion, social mores, or the views of the other branches that its very legitimacy was threatened. When arguments are offered for judicial restraint, *Dred Scott* is typically provided as an example in support. Few decisions were as political as this one (Kutler 1984, 150): It splintered the Democratic Party and helped the emerging Republican Party.

The decision also threatened the judiciary's independence and much of the work that Marshall and Taney had done to strengthen the Court. A newspaper editorial in October 1857 summed up the damage (in language that sounded like Justice Stevens's dissent in *Bush v. Gore*), "The country will feel the consequences of the decision more deeply and more permanently in the loss of confidence in the sound judicial integrity and strictly legal character of their tribunals, than in anything beside; and this, perhaps may well be accounted the greatest political calamity which this country, under our forms of government could sustain" (Witt 1990, 140).

After the decision, the Court suffered through an institutional decline that lasted for more than a generation (Rehnquist 1997, 147). Indeed, President Lincoln felt free enough to ignore a Court decision on habeas corpus. Lincoln was permitted to add seats to the Court, then when Andrew Johnson tried to fill vacancies, Congress abolished the seats.

Substantive Due Process

After the Civil War tore the nation asunder, the Court's decisions, particularly those involving the Fourteenth Amendment, helped rebuild the republic. The Court contributed to the development of economic liberalism by taking governmental restraints off business (Ely 1992; Gillman 1993). The growth of American business could not have occurred without the intervention of the Court and several key decisions. Those decisions did not come without a price, however. Many of those costs were borne by the recently freed slaves.

The scope of judicial review seemed to change late in the nineteenth century. The justices invalidated a number of state and federal laws that violated their sense of justice rather than basing their decision on the intent of the framers. Using their notions of substantive due process led to a dramatic expansion of judicial review and changed the nature of the Fourteenth Amendment (Wolfe 1997, 17–18).

Substantive due process is the doctrine some justices claimed was found in the amendment that says all state legislation is "subject to the scrutiny of the Court." In essence, it allowed the Court to substitute its judgment for that of the legislature. This doctrine was a Court creation. The Court's quintessential statement about substantive due process was in *Lochner v. New York* (1905) when the Court invalidated state legislation designed to protect workers. The Court used the doctrine in defense of property rights, striking down maximum hours and minimum wage provisions because they interfered with the liberty of contract. In dissent, Justice Oliver Wendell Holmes rebuked the majority for inventing a liberty of contract to enforce its own economic laissez-faire philosophy (Schwartz 1993, 190–202). The due process clause became an "activist judicial warrant for passing judgment on the substantive policies of legislative regulations" (Pritchett 1984a, 292). Substantive due process is considered wanton judicial activism and has become discredited doctrine. One of the worst charges that can be leveled at a justice is that he or she is advocating substantive due process.

The Great Depression provided a stark economic context for a Court that was very protective of business. To counteract the economic crisis, President Franklin D. Roosevelt formulated an ambitious agenda labeled the New Deal. The major component of the New Deal was a vast regulatory mechanism designed to curb the excesses of business.

Analysts tend to equate judicial activism with a liberal ideology, but the early New Deal turned that notion on its head. A conservative Court was activist in its attacks on the constitutionality of the New Deal. Roosevelt's election ushered in a new era in American sociopolitical and economic history. Roosevelt presided over a dramatic transformation in the role of the U.S. government. He inaugurated the modern era for the presidency, the government, and the national economy (Neustadt 1976, 192–195). The New Deal provided a new set of issues for the Court to consider.

The election of 1932 has frequently been described as a critical election leading to a partisan realignment. The concept of a realignment refers specifically to the restructuring of the two major political parties, but it goes beyond the party structure: It is a fundamental reconstruction of the political universe. Realignments—dubbed peaceful American revolutions—change the nature of political discourse for the next generation. The era following a critical election is often characterized as the most propitious time for true policy innovation (Sundquist 1983, 26–39). This seemed to be the case in 1933 with the change in regime and changes in political philosophy.

Scholars have long debated whether the Supreme Court responds to changes of the magnitude that accompany a realignment. One school of thought suggests the Court does follow the election returns, particularly when they are emblazoned across the political terrain (Dahl 1957; Funston 1975), while another feels that the Court does not necessarily follow the political branches (Casper 1976; Gates 1992). While a realignment brings a new party to power, the Constitution provides the Court with some insulation from these political trends: The Court's membership is a carryover from the previous political structure. Many of the justices had been selected by the party whose policies were suddenly remnants of a bygone political era and had been overwhelmingly repudiated by the voters.

The history of the Court is marked by occasional self-inflicted wounds, such as the *Dred Scott* decision,[1] that have threatened the Court's very legitimacy. In the mid-1930s, the Court was on such a precipice. The bitterly divided Court's initial response to the New Deal was resistance. In the early period of the New Deal and the partisan realignment, the Court did not follow the election returns and defied the new political order.

In many of the early cases involving New Deal programs, four conservative ideologues—Justices George Sutherland, Willis Van Devanter, James McReynolds, and Pierce Butler—consistently opposed the new policies. These justices, often referred to as the Four Horsemen, needed an additional vote to construct a majority and often got it from the newest member of the Court, Owen Roberts. To make the Court look more unified and stronger, Chief Justice Charles Evans Hughes joined the majority. Public opinion, newspapers, and the elected branches excoriated the Court, particularly focusing on the older conservatives.

In its attempts to preserve the old order and resist the New Deal, the Supreme Court used a variety of devices. The goal was to limit governmental power to regulate business in favor of laissez-faire capitalism. Led by the Four Horsemen, the Court limited federal power by narrowing the interpretation of the Commerce Clause and the authority to tax and spend for the general welfare, and limited state power by reinvigorating the Contracts Clause and using substantive due process (Mason 1979, 40–74). It was a vision of policy goals, not constitutional principles. The Court was accused of acting as a "superlegislature." Perhaps no doctrine better exemplifies the controversy over judicial policymaking than substantive due process. The Court used this doctrine to review state legislation that was considered "arbitrary, unfair, or unjust." Of course, it was left to a majority of the Court to define what constituted "arbitrary, unfair, or unjust."

President Roosevelt, with a resounding electoral mandate in his pocket, proposed a "Court-packing plan," ostensibly to help the beleaguered, overworked "nine old men." The thinly veiled plan to alter the Court's working majority failed to pass Senate scrutiny or attract public support, but when Roberts and Hughes left the Four Horsemen and began upholding the building blocks of the New Deal (the "switch in time that saved nine"), further crises were averted. By the 1937–1938 period, the Court finally moved into step with the reigning political order in economic matters.

The Court that resisted the New Deal was activist in a number of ways: It tampered with statutory provisions, ran roughshod over the attempts of elected officials at all levels to stem the economic problems that beset the nation, created novel constitutional principles to fulfill its policy goals, and attacked precedents.

It was one of the few instances of full-scale activism and aggressive policymaking across the board and placed the Court in institutional jeopardy. The Court had put itself above Congress, the president, and the state legislatures. The activism of the period was evident in the numbers. The Court struck down 35 federal laws in the period between *Lochner* and "the switch in time"—almost a dozen more than in the preceding century. More revealing is that the Court declared more than 350 state laws and municipal ordinances unconstitutional, over 100 more than in the nineteenth century (Baum 2001, 197–199). The Court had risked its institutional legitimacy, its only resource. Faced with active opposition from the other branches, the Court retreated.

The Court's ultimate decision to leave the foundation of the New Deal intact left the Court in a curious position. Having capitulated, the Court might have relegated itself to a subordinate role, rubber-stamping the prerogatives of the elected branches. Rather, the Court used the opportunity as a point of departure for its own transformation and adopted a new role. In a manner reminiscent of the Marshall Court, the Hughes Court had to reestablish its legitimacy and proper niche in the governmental structure. Eventually, Roosevelt had the opportunity to appoint a number of justices. In a direct, if delayed, sense, the partisan realignment percolated to the judiciary. The New Deal, which affected the presidency, Congress, and intergovernmental relations, now had an impact on the authority and role of the Supreme Court (Pacelle 1991, 47–51).

The Preferred Position Doctrine: Selective Judicial Activism

As a result of the events that pushed the Court to the brink of conflict with Congress and the president and threatened the Court's institutional legitimacy, a majority of the justices eventually supported a new context for judicial decision-making. To reinvent its institutional role, Justice Harlan Fiske Stone suggested that the Court adopt the preferred position doctrine. Stone offered it in footnote four of an economic regulatory decision, *United States v. Carolene Products*. The preferred position doctrine advocated a double standard by which economic cases would be accorded less rigorous review, while individual rights cases would receive more exacting judicial scrutiny. In other words, the Court would exhibit judicial restraint in economic matters and activism in civil liberties and civil rights (Pacelle 1991, 51–54). This was a reversal of the previous period, during which the Court was activist in overturning economic legislation but exercised restraint in civil liberties. Some on the Court, such as Justice Felix Frankfurter, found the doctrine abhorrent because it smacked of the type of judicial activism that pushed the Court to the precipice during the early New Deal (Silverstein 1983).

The development of the preferred position doctrine and the protection of individual rights was a path with potential pitfalls. While the nation recovered from World War II, an ideological cold war began to consume policymakers. The Court seemed to feel the effects, especially in First Amendment cases that dealt with the espousal of unpopular ideas. The Vinson Court (1946–1953) was reluctant to advance the causes of civil liberties and civil rights too abruptly (Pritchett 1954, 3–4), so advocates of the preferred position often found themselves in the minority during that time.

The activism of the preferred position doctrine reached its zenith during the Warren Court (1953–1969). His success in marshaling a unanimous opinion in *Brown v. Board of Education* (making it illegal to segregate white and black students) was a clear sign that Chief Justice Earl Warren would bring impressive leadership skills to his stewardship (Schwartz 1983). Under his direction, the Court presided over a constitutional revolution. The Court changed the face of the law with *Brown*, which reinvented the Fourteenth Amendment and overturned *Plessy v. Ferguson*, as well as with a vast expansion of the First Amendment and a due process revolution. Further aggressive policymaking was reflected in the process of selective incorporation (applying portions of the Bill of Rights to the states through the Fourteenth Amendment); the Warren Court applied portions of the Fourth, Fifth, Sixth, and Eighth Amendments to the states.

In these and other areas, the Warren Court issued decisions that dismantled a number of precedents, changed legislative provisions, exercised judicial review, and dramatically expanded portions of the Bill of Rights and the Constitution. The Warren Court struck down 20 federal laws and 200 state and local laws (Baum 2001, 197–199). The Court had pragmatic reasons for the multifaceted constitutional revolution. The additional constitutional provisions would protect the *Brown* decision. Expanded civil rights protection would extend beyond the classroom to other parts of everyday life. The process of selective incorporation of the Bill of Rights had a not-so-hidden agenda of protecting potential black defendants in the South. The Court took another forceful step in protecting defendants by issuing a radical reinterpretation of the writ of habeas corpus. The writ, in the language of the Constitution, was originally designed to ensure that an accused person be brought to trial at some point. The Warren Court reinvented the writ, allowing defendants who lost in the state courts to have a second chance by applying for a writ of habeas corpus to have the case retried in the federal courts. Once again, this would serve to protect African American defendants in the South (Pacelle 1991, 182–189; Powe 2000, 198–199).

The Warren Court also ordered states and Congress to reapportion their legislative districts to reflect population changes (I will examine reapportionment more fully in Chapter 4). The result of the Court's decisions in this area was to give the cities more seats and thus more power in state legislatures and Congress. That would presumably translate to more urban programs that would help African Americans.

The Warren Court articulated a constitutional philosophy that elevated individual rights over governmental power and human rights over property rights (Justice 1997b, 305). The Court was willing to use the Constitution when it supported the justices' conception of good law. When the Constitution did not provide the authority to do that, the Court would interpret the document more broadly to create the authority. The Warren Court was not shy about abandoning precedent, overturning state legislation, expanding statutory interpretation, and utilizing judicial review. When the elected branches of government refused to address certain issues, the Supreme Court seemed willing to step into the vacuum.

The Warren Court was not particularly popular. Public opinion was strongly opposed to many of the decisions. The civil rights decisions rankled the South; decisions that protected the rights of Communists and freed criminals angered the whole nation. The Warren Court made unpopular decisions that were perceived as antireligious, such as decisions to ban teacher-led prayer or devotional readings in school. Billboards in the South urged the impeachment of Earl Warren. Gerald Ford led two attempts to impeach Justice William Douglas, an admitted activist. The Court became a campaign issue and a whipping boy for politicians (Powe 2000, 262).

With the evolution of the preferred position doctrine, the nature of judicial activism changed in significant ways. *Brown* was a critical step in the Court's support of massive remedial power. In terms of constitutional interpretation, the Court supported broad general principles in an open-ended fashion. The modern form of activism has been identified as more legislative in character (Wolfe 1997, 26–27). In essence, the Court is accused of acting like a legislature and making the law. The Court was willing to extend relief to whole classes of citizens and definable groups. The Court also went beyond the creation or expansion of rights to constructing remedies such as busing to correct past abuses.

The Warren Court made it easier for litigants to get into court (see Chapter 4 for more on this). Cases have to be properly brought to the Supreme Court in order to be decided. In the past half-century, the Court has been willing to decide cases, even if the case has some defects. Notions of judicial deference to the elected branches had been modified as well. In the area of civil rights and individual liberties, the Courts presumed that state and federal laws were unconstitutional.

The Burger and Rehnquist Courts: Return to Restraint?

The Burger Court (1969–1986) was an important bridge between the Warren and Rehnquist Courts. The Burger Court did not initiate a full-blown retreat or "counterrevolution" (Urofsky 1991; Baum 1989). In some areas, such as equal protection, the Burger Court decisions were the next logical step from the decisions of the Warren Court. The Burger Court was the first to address directly issues such as gender discrimination. Decisions supporting broad remedies like affirmative action and busing and creating the right to an abortion were issued during Warren Burger's tenure. On the other hand, the Burger Court was somewhat less expansive of First Amendment rights and retreated from the Warren Court pronouncements in criminal procedure (Schwartz 1998).

The Burger Court was forced, in many ways, to work within the contours shaped by the Warren Court. It is often the nature of Supreme Court policymaking that precedents, even if not rigidly adhered to, must at least be considered, distinguished, and incrementally undermined if they are to be rejected. The Burger Court applied the brakes to some of the expansion of rights that occurred during the Warren Court and began retreats that have accelerated during the Rehnquist Court. The Burger Court, however, directly overturned very few precedents.

Despite the varied mix of ideologies and philosophies, or perhaps because of them, there was no one dominant political theory guiding doctrinal construction and decisionmaking during the Burger Court. Rather, a balancing approach seemed to carry the day in many of the decisions (Schwartz 1990)—partially a result of the pragmatic nature of the so-called swing justices. At various times referred to as the "fluid four" or the "fluid five," the middle of the Burger Court often provided the key votes and thus control over the tone and content of opinions. The result was often criticized for not providing guidance to lower courts and for failing to develop a coherent overarching philosophy. The balancing approach was used to counter the preferred position approach, which still had supporters and favorable precedents from the Warren Court.

The Burger Court was a combination of judicial activism and restraint. Indeed, the supposedly conservative Burger Court pushed doctrine to the left in a number of areas (Maltz 2000, 1–2). The Court continued to expand the Constitution, broadening the reach of the Fourteenth Amendment. Under Burger, and sometimes over his dissents, the Court created reproductive rights, built a high wall of separation between church and state, and expanded the use of remedies such as busing and affirmative action. The later Burger Court, with changes in membership, increasingly deferred to the elected branches, followed precedent, and tried to limit expansive views of the Constitution. Indeed, if the Burger Court did not induce a wholesale retreat from the Warren Court, it created the conditions for the more conservative Rehnquist Court (Schwartz 1998, 268–269).

The Burger Court struck down more federal laws than the activist Warren Court. The Rehnquist Court, despite its claims to be restraintist, has declared almost as many laws unconstitutional as its two predecessors combined.[2] The Burger Court struck down more state laws and local ordinances than any previous tribunal. The Rehnquist Court, reflecting its respect for federalism, has dramatically reduced the number of state and local laws held unconstitutional (Baum 2001, 196–199).

The Rehnquist Court (1971–present) has retreated from many of the precedents and policies of the Warren Court (Savage 1992; Simon 1995). Yet in an important symbolic decision, Justices Anthony Kennedy and David Souter joined Justice Sandra Day O'Connor in *Planned Parenthood v. Casey*, refusing to overturn *Roe v. Wade*.[3] The decision is the quintessential expression of judicial restraint. The three justices wrote, in effect, that it was important that the law was settled. They claimed that despite their reservations about *Roe*, the weight of *stare decisis* (precedent) argued for its continuance. Despite the well-publicized failure to overturn *Roe* and the *Lemon* test (which the Supreme Court uses in freedom of religion cases), conservatives have scored some impressive victories, rolling back school desegregation and affirmative action, placing restrictions on a woman's right to choose, and suggesting a new balance for federalism.

More significant for the state of law and for the legacy that is bequeathed to future courts is the fact that the Rehnquist Court appears to be forming a revised philosophy to guide its work (Kahn 1994, 255–260; Yarbrough 2000, chapter 4).[4]

Chief Justice William Rehnquist has advocated avoiding controversial issues to force the elected branches to deal with them. Certainly, that philosophy reflects some components of deference and judicial restraint. In addition, there appears to be a rejection of the principles that have served as the foundation for the double standard—that civil liberties be held in a preferred position. The resignations of Justices William Brennan and Thurgood Marshall meant that for the first time in fifty years, there was no real proponent of the preferred position approach on the Court. Given the near critical mass of conservatives and the longevity of precedents and philosophies once they become entrenched, the Rehnquist Court could establish the context for judicial policy for the next half-century (Pacelle 1995).

Members of the Rehnquist Court have argued that they support judicial restraint. Indeed, the Court seems to do so in cases involving civil liberties and civil rights. The justices tend to uphold state laws and policies that conflict with individual rights and liberties. However, the Court seems to have a decidedly activist approach when dealing with state laws that involve economic policies. The Rehnquist Court has reinvented the Takings Clause and the Commerce Clause of the Constitution. To a degree, then, there is a new double standard that elevates economic rights over individual rights (Yarbrough 2000).

Overall, the Rehnquist Court has engaged in considerable activism. Some see a decision like *Bush v. Gore* as being activist, despite the Court's pronouncements about exercising judicial restraint. The Court also appears willing to abdicate its traditional role as a protector of minority rights (Justice 1997b, 305). The Rehnquist Court has read the Bill of Rights and most provisions of the Constitution rather narrowly. It has not shown the traditional respect for precedent expected of a restraintist Court. Justice Scalia has argued that overturning a precedent that was improperly conceived in the first place is the ultimate act of judicial restraint.

Judicial restraint in civil liberties and civil rights carries a risk. For more than a half-century, the Court has been considered the protector of individual rights. As an unelected branch of government whose members serve for life, the Court is theoretically insulated from the political winds, which would allow it to stand up for minority rights. If the Court develops restraint that manifests itself in deference to the elected branches and a narrow construction of statutes and the Constitution, then it risks abdicating this role. If the elected branches are not vigilant in protecting minority rights, then there is no protection for individuals and groups who do not have recourse to the other branches of government.

Conclusion

At its inception, clearly the Supreme Court was the least dangerous branch of government. At times in its history, though, the Court has been part of the so-called imperial judiciary. Members of the Rehnquist Court, aware of the reputation of its predecessors, have argued that the Court should adopt a new role that limits its authority and power.

Institutions are shaped by the formal powers of the body, the interplay of actors as they seek to realize their goals, the settings in which they act and may help to shape, and the historical context in which their decisions are set (Aldrich 1994, 227). The Court is governed by a set of rules, but it shaped its own powers over time. The Court created its most important power: judicial review. The justices have the authority to enforce the institutional rules stringently or be flexible in their application.

While the institution and the rules shape the behavior of the Supreme Court, history played an enormous role as well. The intersection of the combination of justices, the rules, and historical situations led to significant changes in the power of the Supreme Court and to changing notions of judicial activism and restraint.

Chapter 1 examined four modes of judicial activism and aggressive policymaking: overturning precedent, undertaking judicial review, and expanding statutory provisions and constitutional provisions. Traditional notions of judicial activism involve the Court's treatment of its own precedents and its exercise of judicial review. Modern judicial activism involves the expansion or contraction of statutory or constitutional interpretation, and is marked by use of broad remedies and sweeping policy.

This chapter looked at five periods when the Court exercised one or more of those modes of activism, which often led to challenges to the Court's authority and legitimacy. At issue is how to evaluate the appropriate role of the Supreme Court and when it should adopt judicial restraint. In subsequent chapters, three dimensions to the dilemma of the appropriate use of power will be considered: democratic theory, institutional constraints, and questions of judicial capacity.

The following gives some examples of the three dimensions. The Court in the period 1933–1937 struck down large portions of the New Deal in the face of a realignment and overwhelming congressional majorities, raising concerns with democratic theory, the subject of Chapter 3. Similarly, the Rehnquist Court's perceived retreat from the protection of civil rights and liberties has implications for democratic theory. The activism of the Warren Court was marked by, among other things, the loosening of restraints on litigants. The Court would accept cases even if they had jurisdictional defects, raising the institutional dimension of the dilemma, which will be examined in Chapter 4. The aggressive policymaking of the Burger Court in mandating sweeping remedies such as busing and affirmative action raises questions of judicial capacity, which will be considered in Chapter 5.

In addition to the three institutional-level dimensions, there is an individual dimension to the dilemma that evaluates the factors justices use when they decide a case. I examine that in Chapter 6. Just as the appropriate exercise of activism and restraint changes with the times, so does the impact of the various dimensions. That is the subject of the rest of this book.

Notes

1. The *Dred Scott* decision led to the crisis that provoked a previous realignment.

2. Baum (2001, 196–198) notes that in the 1960–1990 period, many of the record number of laws struck down by the Court were relatively minor or very old laws. Since 1995, though, the Rehnquist Court has struck down a large number of laws, many of which have been quite consequential.

3. This reluctance to overturn important, controversial precedents was manifested in *Lee v. Weisman,* involving an invocation at a school assembly, when Justice Kennedy provided the fifth vote to uphold the *Lemon* test, despite his previous objections to that standard. During the 1999 term, the Rehnquist Court had the opportunity to overturn *Miranda,* but refused in *Dickerson v. United States.*

4. The philosophical charge to the right may have had costs. The stark positions adopted by Scalia and Thomas may have chased conservatives Kennedy and O'Connor to the middle of the Court. When the Court has had the opportunity to overturn some of the liberal precedents, those advocates have been unable to muster the votes. Scalia's opinions have taken on an increasingly personal tone as he has criticized O'Connor and others (Simon 1995).

3

The Democratic Dimension of the Dilemma: Unelected Policymaking

O_N THE FIRST TUESDAY after the first Monday of November of even-numbered years, American citizens flock to the polls (although in dwindling numbers in the last few decades). Ideally, they vote for the candidates or party that best reflect their policy views. Winners hope the election gives them a mandate to enact their policy goals into law. If the newly elected officeholders fail to represent the views of the electorate, they can be voted out of office.

On the first Monday of each October, amid much less fanfare, the nine justices of the Supreme Court convene to begin their term. During the year, the justices will hear a number of important cases that will have significant policy implications. If their decisions are at odds with public opinion, there is little recourse available. They do not face the voters.

The question of what role unelected judges should play in charting the course of American public policy is, in a nutshell, the democratic dimension of the dilemma surrounding the appropriate role of the Supreme Court. The undemocratic nature of the Court is a normative argument for judicial restraint. Consider the two examples that follow:

Can a state write a nondenominational prayer for students to recite at the beginning of each school day? The prayer might run afoul of the First Amendment prohibition against the establishment of religion. At the same time, public support for school prayer and the introduction of some religious practices into public schools is overwhelming. This puts the Supreme Court in the difficult position of having to make a decision in the face of strong public support for a suspect policy. Ultimately, in *Engel v. Vitale* (1962), the Court decided to ignore public sentiment and held that the state should not be in the business of writing or proscribing a prayer. In doing so, the Court continued to erect a high wall of separation between church and state that many felt was very different from what the framers intended.

Can the government pass a law that bans burning the American flag, the symbol of freedom, as an expression of protest? The Supreme Court issued an unpopular decision in *Texas v. Johnson* (1989), holding that flag burning was protected speech under the First Amendment. In response to overwhelming public criticism of the decision, President Bush signed a measure passed by the House and Senate to protect the flag. Now the Supreme Court was in a delicate position. Would it stand up to the elected branches of government and strong public support and reinstate its decision or bow to popular will? In *United States v. Eichmann* (1990), the Court reinforced its earlier decision and declared the Flag Protection Act of 1989 unconstitutional.

Each of these examples involved the democratic dimension of the dilemma for the Supreme Court. The Court made decisions that created strong public reaction and declared popular laws unconstitutional. These decisions raise some of the most enduring questions of American politics: How should unelected justices treat the popular will and the desires of the elected branches? If the Court rejects the position of the elected branches, is it showing contempt for democratic principles? If the Court defers to the elected branches, will the rights of minorities be sufficiently protected? These issues will be considered in this chapter.

Perhaps the questions raised above are most salient when considering minority rights and individual liberties. The protection of the rights of individuals and minorities has always presented difficult questions for a democracy. How does a society founded on majoritarian, democratic principles balance the rights of individuals and minorities with the duty of the state to maintain order? What mechanisms are available to prevent what Alexis de Tocqueville called "the tyranny of the majority"? In the vernacular, Ronald Reagan asked the rhetorical question, "Hasn't something gone haywire when this great Constitution of ours is invoked to allow Nazis and Ku Klux Klansmen to march, but it supposedly prevents our children from saying a simple prayer in school?"

Studies show most Americans agreed with Reagan and his successor, George Bush, who made political capital by bashing groups such as the American Civil Liberties Union that seek to protect the liberties of individuals. Even Bill Clinton, thought to be liberal, supported severe restrictions on the Internet, advertising, and television programming—issues all carrying important First Amendment questions. Members of Congress have repeatedly lined up to support a constitutional amendment to punish flag burning, despite two Supreme Court decisions that placed such protests under the protection of the First Amendment.

Americans have long held ambivalent feelings about the courts: They want courts to protect minority rights and defer to the elected branches of government (Rosenberg 1991, 3). While those two desires may complement each other at times, they are often incompatible. This incompatibility is the essence of the democratic dilemma.

Certainly, there needs to be some mechanism to check the excesses of the majority or the elected branches. The Constitution and the Bill of Rights were designed for just that purpose, and the Supreme Court plays an important role in checking the other branches. When, though, is it appropriate for the Court to intercede and restrict the other branches? Proponents of judicial activism and judicial restraint agree that the elected branches of government cannot cross the outer limits of their authority without being subject to judicial intervention. However, there is a world of disagreement concerning the location of those limits (Wallace 1997, 164).

Gerald Rosenberg (1991, 2) notes that "for many, part of what makes American democracy exceptional is that it includes the world's most powerful court system, protecting minorities and defending liberty, in the face of opposition from the democratically elected branches." Historically, this role of protector of minorities has been advocated by some members of the Court since 1938 (the concept appeared in footnote four in the *Carolene Products* decision; [Pacelle 1991, 50]), but it has not been acceptable to all justices and has been undermined since the 1980s. Critics have argued that elected legislative majorities in the states and the national government have greater authority to ensure order, and the courts should be reluctant to interfere with that authority.

It all comes down to whether or not unelected judges should make public policy. Unfortunately, there is no easy answer to the question. Before this question is addressed more directly, consider the context the Supreme Court faces with regard to democratic theory. The democratic values that underpin the system may be significantly greater than the practical influence of democracy.

Democratic Theory and the Supreme Court

The United States is nominally a democracy. Today, suffrage is the broadest it has ever been. Voters can elect the president (indirectly through the electoral college), representatives, and senators, as well as executives and representatives at the state and local levels. Democratic theory and judicial restraint suggest that if there are policy issues or problems, it is up to the elected branches and the voters to make changes. It is a question of accountability and responsibility. Voters have the opportunity to throw the rascals out if they are displeased with the policies emerging from Congress or the state legislatures. The Constitution created a federalist system, giving significant authority to the states as well as the central government. Proponents of judicial restraint would argue further that federal judges, in particular, should respect the state political process and not interfere with the policies of the elected officials.

The Supreme Court is constitutionally removed from the democratic process. There is very little connection between the voters and the Supreme Court. The nomination and confirmation process are the primary means by which democratic values are infused in the Court (O'Brien 1997, 2). While presidential campaigns are seldom contested on the issue of appointments to the Supreme Court, voters elect presidents who may have the opportunity to nominate justices. Even if the Court itself is not an election issue, the new president gets a mandate of sorts to nominate individuals who reflect his judicial philosophy. Once on the Court, the justices are even farther removed from the public.

Democratic principles, which are critical in a theoretical sense, carry some inherent protections. There are strong normative reasons for the Court to follow democratic designs. The president and members of Congress are restrained by the ballot box, safeguards that do not extend to the judicial branch. Justice Harlan Fiske Stone noted that the only check on the justices' "exercise of power is [their] own sense of self-restraint" (O'Brien 1997, 1). There are also practical reasons for paying attention to democratic principles. If the Court is in step with public opinion, then its decisions will not be threatened by the other branches of government. The prospects for implementation are enhanced when the policies are supported by the branches with the power and resources the Court lacks (Rosenberg 1991, 15).

Sometimes courts act in a countermajoritarian way—against the clear wishes of the majority. History shows that there have been times when the Supreme Court has substituted its judgment for that of the elected branches. In some cases, the elected branches clearly stepped over the line constitutionally and the Supreme Court's decision was more than justified. Other times, though, the elected branches did not appear to violate the Constitution, and yet the Court reacted as if they had—which poses a significant risk for the Court if it frequently acts in such a manner. The Court's power rests on its legitimacy, the belief that its decisions are correct and proper. A Court that continually ignores the elected branches or public opinion can undermine the respect its power is based upon. A Court that tries to grab power and make public policy that continually contravenes the elected branches and public wishes risks its institutional position. An aggressive judiciary also dilutes the power of the other branches and undermines their legitimacy.

How far should the justices stray from precedent, the law, and the Constitution? Table 3.1 lists the arguments supporting restraint due to democratic concerns and countervailing claims considered in this chapter. Those who subscribe to a model of majoritarian democracy argue that justices should confine themselves to the law, precedents, statutory language, and the provisions of the Constitution and avoid the inclination to interject personal values into decisions. They would say that it is up to the elected branches to make changes in the law. The practical recommendations for judges is that they should always hesitate to declare statutes unconstitutional and demonstrate caution in modifying or supplementing statutes when construing them. The bottom line is that courts

● ●

TABLE 3.1 Supreme Court Policymaking and Democratic Theory

Problems and Consequences for Court	Countervailing Arguments
Elected branches have more legitimacy	Court is deliberately undemocratic
Lack of accountability/responsibility	Elected branches are not democratic
Saps democracy	Pluralism
Diminishes elected branches	Practical realities of politics
Exposes the court	Protect minority rights

Source: Richard Pacelle.

should exercise judicial restraint and make as little policy as possible (Wallace 1997, 169).

The concerns connected to the democratic dimension do not forbid the Court from making policy or from striking down the handiwork of the elected branches. But such concerns urge the justices to be reluctant to resort to that very often. Those who argue for judicial restraint due to democratic principles say that there should be clear standards for the justices to use when they take the extraordinary step of overruling the other branches. They urge the justices to focus on democratic values or apply some neutral principles that would permit them to substitute their judgment for that of the elected branches. The justices should not enforce their own wills, but those of the framers and the will of the people as reflected in the Constitution. These issues are examined in Chapter 6.

There is some judicial activism that is consistent with democratic principles. If the Court overturns a precedent that has outlived its usefulness or has clearly fallen from public favor, then it is acting within the democratic framework. Civil rights, for example, was an issue whose time had come, and the Court began to undermine *Plessy* to accommodate that, beginning in the 1930s and culminating in *Brown* (1954).

Any new democratic theory necessitating changes in judicial interpretation should come not from the justices but from the elected branches of government and popular will. Even Justice Hugo Black, who demonstrated his share of judicial activism, argued that "when a 'political theory' embodied in our Constitution becomes outdated, it seems to me that a majority of the nine members of the Court are not only without constitutional power but are far less qualified to

choose a new constitutional political theory than the people of this country"
(O'Brien 1997, 137).

Policymaking Against Majority Will

Obviously, any judicial decision, no matter how mundane, makes policy to some
degree. Proponents of judicial restraint argue that basing decisions on democratic values is so important that judges should be very reluctant to take decisions
away from the elected representatives (Wallace 1997, 165). Where are democratic
values found? Some analysts claim there are shared "neutral" values that define
American government, and the Court should pay attention to those. Chief Justice
Rehnquist (1997, 152) believed that democratic values are best discovered
through the democratic branches of government—a recipe for judicial restraint.

In keeping with democratic principles, some see the growth of judicial power
as troubling because of its source, rather than its consequences. Opponents of activism often argue that judicial policy is not only undemocratic but profoundly
antidemocratic. They maintain power has shifted to the courts because of a distrust of the people (Hickok and McDowell 1993). It is the fear of democracy and
majoritarian impulses that has created the notion of the Court as nine platonic
guardians who are infallible, not because of their collective judgment, but because
of their position as members of the highest court and their insulation from tenure
considerations.

The Court finds itself at odds with democratic values when it makes policy,
rather than letting that policy come from the elected branches. In these instances,
one could argue that popular government is supplanted by judicial decree
(O'Brien 1997, xi). That can occur when the Court's decisions are in marked contrast to the public's desires or when the Court "invents" a new right or "finds" one
in the Constitution. In the latter case, which is an example of "modern" judicial
activism, when the justices make a constitutional decision, the only chance of reversing that decision is getting the near-impossible supermajority needed to pass
a constitutional amendment. Proponents of democratic theory say that such dramatic changes in the law must come from the elected branches (McKeever 1993,
36). It is the job of legislatures to author laws that reflect changing times.

The Court makes policy when it interprets statutory provisions more broadly
or narrowly than the legislature intended. It is a truism that all laws need interpretation. The political process, with its multiple veto points,[1] ensures that laws have
vague provisions. Who should be charged with the interpretation of those laws?
As many have argued, he who interprets the law is the true lawmaker (Miller
1982a, 170). Traditionally, that responsibility and power has fallen to the courts;

in effect, that passes important policymaking authority to the courts, even if that is not the intention.

Perhaps the most troubling notion of the Court's work may arise when the justices declare an act of Congress or the president unconstitutional. At these junctures, unelected justices are substituting their judgments and conceptions of the Constitution and policy for those of the duly elected representatives of the people. Many argue that judicial review is countermajoritarian and, to the extent that it determines public policy, it is undemocratic. Typically, this is manifested in judicial activism. Judicial restraintists, on the other hand, would say that the courts should follow the elected branches and the dictates of public opinion.

Democratic theory does not look at the substance of the decision, which can change with the times. The process is more important than the decision itself. The locus of power is important also. Proponents of democratic theory say that it is better to have a majority make a mistake than to have courts substituting their judgment for the elected officials. A mistake by the elected branches presumably can be corrected more easily than one by the courts. On theoretical grounds, many argue that the majority has earned the right to be wrong (Wallace 1997, 166). Judicial restraint suggests deference even when the judge feels the elected branches have erred. The voters have given the elected branches the authority to make decisions and can rescind it at the next election. There is no recourse for the voters when the Supreme Court oversteps its bounds.

Democratic theory holds that judicial activism has negative consequences for the judiciary and the system more broadly. Broad policymaking that is out of step with the elected branches or public opinion places the Court at risk. Institutionally, the Court must rely on the executive and legislative branches to reinforce and implement its decisions. If the president and Congress oppose the decision, it could cost the Court its legitimacy. Congress and the president are more likely to be recalcitrant when the decision is unpopular with the public. Overreliance on the Court can be detrimental to the judiciary as well for reasons that are tied to institutional concerns examined in Chapters 4 and 5. The willingness of the Court to expand its authority implies that the elected branches can be circumvented. Courts have been an important resource for groups, which can use them to end run the other branches of government. Civil rights groups, for instance, used the Supreme Court because Congress had blocked any initiatives. There were some good democratic reasons for the Court to be active in this area. Arguably, it was minorities in Congress, Southern Democrats, who used legislative procedures such as committee rules and filibusters to thwart majority rule. The Court can also be used to thwart the will of the majority. After Franklin Roosevelt and Congress orchestrated a remarkable package of legislative initiatives with the solid support of the public, the Supreme Court eviscerated key provisions of the

New Deal. It was clear that business and economic interests could use votes from five or six justices to hold huge electoral majorities at bay.

The Supreme Court's reaction to the early New Deal represented the classic case of judicial activism. The Court's majority, a remnant of a past period, was holding an entire set of programs hostage, ignoring the public and the mandate given to the elected branches. Like a few other notable expressions of judicial activism, this one was considered a "self-inflicted wound" that almost cost the Court dearly. As it was, the Court suffered some short-term damage.

The legitimacy of the Supreme Court depends on the appropriateness of the exercise of its power. Democratic theory suggests that success in the legislature or elected branches is likely to be more enduring and legitimate than it is in the courts (McKeever 1993, 279). Legislative and executive policies carry more legitimacy because voters and subsequent legislatures and executives would have, at least implicitly, refused to overturn the existing initiatives.

Overuse of judicial review and aggressive policymaking by the Court raise public disapproval or invite rebuke from the other branches. For its own institutional protection, the Court must take account of public opinion. When the Court opposes the position of the elected branches or the boundaries imposed by public opinion, it puts its legitimacy at risk (Fisher 1988, 13). Ultimately, legitimacy is the Court's most precious and finite resource. While such concerns can be categorized as part of the democratic dilemma, they are tied to the institutional and capacity concerns, which are examined in the next two chapters.

Many of the Warren Court's criminal procedure decisions, which were said to "handcuff the police," were unpopular with the public. The decision banning state-sponsored school prayer was opposed by two-thirds of the public (Powe 2000, 186–199). The Rehnquist Court's decision to change the standards for evaluating free exercise of religion claims in *Employment Division, Department of Human Resources of Oregon v. Smith* was met with broadscale disapproval from religious groups and from Congress (Epstein and Walker 1998b, 130).

Review Compatible with Democratic Values

Too much reliance on the courts can sap democracy and diminish the authority of the elected branches. Some argue that a society that relies on courts and judges to make the important political and moral decisions is a society that has lost touch with what self-government or elected government is all about. Many charge that the Court has taken the truly important questions away from the citizens. If groups can achieve their policy goals through the courts, they do not need to be concerned with the democratic engines of government. A Court willing to exercise judicial review and strike down policies passed by the elected branches fosters and encourages disrespect for those institutions. In addition, some maintain that the Court's expanded power emphasizes the weaknesses of the elected branches and may depress voting turnout (Hickok and McDowell 1993, 219–221).

The issue is not black and white, however. Frequent and aggressive use of judicial review would seem to underline the undemocratic nature of the Court. On the other hand, if the Court exercises too much restraint or deference and makes infrequent use of judicial review, it would represent an abdication of judicial power. After all, there are occasions when the elected branches have clearly overstepped their boundaries. If the Supreme Court is perceived as unwilling or unable to do anything of substance, it risks being considered weak or irrelevant and could lose legitimacy. If the Court consistently did little or nothing, citizens would view it as powerless.

Robert Bork (1990, 3, 9), whose nomination to the Supreme Court was rejected by the Senate in 1987, refers to the wholesale creation of rights by unelected justices as "heresy." He argues that the Constitution has been transformed from the major mechanism for limiting arbitrary governmental power into the source for arbitrary judicial power. Even defenders of broad judicial power admit that the growth of individual rights grew out of an undemocratic process. However, they claim that the ends justify the means: that undemocratic decisionmaking actually strengthened democracy (Epp 1998, 4). Reapportioning legislatures, opening channels of political debate, protecting freedom of the press, and extending voting rights were the results of Supreme Court decisions, which expanded democratic values.

Before judicial activism can be dismissed as incompatible with democratic values, five countervailing arguments must be addressed. First, the Constitution specifically set the courts up to be an undemocratic check on the other branches of government. Second, one could argue America is hardly a democracy, and holding the Court to a high standard is hypocritical. Third, many scholars think all the theories of democracy and representative government are so far removed from the practical reality of American politics and government that they no longer can serve as an adequate guide for evaluating the elected branches or the policymaking process. Fourth, some claim that pluralism is a better explanation for the American political system and, as such, the Court is another point of access for citizens and groups. Finally, due to its insulation from the electoral process, the Court may be the only branch that can protect the rights of minorities against possible tyranny of the majority (Justice 1997a, 152–153).

Deliberately Undemocratic

The exhortations against judicial policymaking often gloss over the fact that the Supreme Court was deliberately insulated from popular control. Article III of the Constitution specifically removed the judicial functions of government from democratic influence. As Alexander Hamilton wrote in *The Federalist Papers*, the Court was set up to be independent of the people. The Bill of Rights, which the justices are supposed to interpret, was designed to be countermajoritarian as well (Justice 1997a, 154).

What is unclear, however, is how much authority the third branch of government is supposed to have. Neither the nature nor the scope of judicial power is defined in the Constitution, which did not appear to grant the Supreme Court much power. The document, then, is an inadequate grant of power. As Chapter 4 will show, the Court had to assert power for itself. The Court claimed in 1803 in *Marbury v. Madison* that it had the power to interpret the Constitution and to nullify acts of the elected branches. The uncertain foundation for those powers has been an argument for judicial restraint.

The Constitution was framed with the clear intention of limiting the potential of unfettered democracy. The other branches were mistrusted. Experience with an oppressive executive before the Revolution and widespread distrust of state legislatures during the period the Articles of Confederation served as the form of government played a role in the creation of checks and balances (Wallace 1997, 164). Article III specifically removed one of the central functions of government from democratic influence.

Judicial review was not fully understood by the framers. Chief Justice Marshall expanded judicial power and helped create the controversy over the role of an unelected Court. In addition to the creation of judicial review over federal laws, Marshall established the precedent that federal courts could review state laws. This was controversial at the time and continued to be so as the Supreme Court expanded the exercise of that power. The Warren Court reorganized Southern schools in *Brown* and made states abide by a number of provisions of the Bill of Rights. Oliver Wendell Holmes argued that American government could exist quite easily without judicial review of the president and Congress, but the nation could not survive if the Supreme Court could not review state actions. In general, the power of judicial review placed the Court on a more equal footing with the executive and legislative branches.

If one subscribes to the belief that the Constitution is an evolving grant of power, then the power of judicial review and judicial interpretation are important components of a living Constitution. At the same time, the exercise of active judicial review seems to contradict democratic principles. It permits the Court to substitute its judgment for that of the elected branches of government. Indeed, judicial power to nullify a law is a clear restriction on the power of a duly constituted majority to govern the nation. Justice Robert Jackson (1997, 27–28) noted it is a necessity because unrestricted majority rule leaves minorities unprotected. The judiciary was created as an "auxiliary precaution" against the abuse of governmental power and the potential excesses of an overbearing majority. As David O'Brien (1997, 5) claims, "Judicial review is essential to the promise and performance of a free government."

To Arthur Miller, perhaps the most forceful advocate of judicial activism, the Court fulfills the most basic requirement of the Madisonian system. According to Madison, the task of government was to control the people and to control itself. The Court would become the primary vehicle for the latter. Miller argued that if judicial review did not exist, some institutional device would have to be invented to take its place. There has always been a tension between popular elected government and judicial review. One cannot expect government to control itself or politicians to control themselves. Some would say it is preferable to have an unelected institution exert this control over elected officials and government. It is the role of the Court to impose some legal limits to arbitrary power (Miller 1982a, 172).

Ultimately, one could argue that though the Court is not a democratic institution, it can contribute to the overall enterprise, holding the "democratic" branches accountable for their decisions (Miller 1982a, 173). Some issues, such as civil rights, freedom of religion, and freedom of speech, can serve as an important justification for insulating the judiciary from popular control and influence.

There are practical considerations tied to democratic theory as well. Proponents of a more active judiciary refute the argument that the only positions that are authoritative are those that are passed by a majority. They assert that a slavish adherence to judicial restraint can become judicial abdication. Activists argue there is no guarantee that the majority is invested with some innate quality of being correct just because it has pure numbers on its side. In particular, they maintain that "the will of a transient majority should not be allowed to trump enduring constitutional values or hard won constitutional rights" (Justice 1997a, 155–158). This is a critical point, because the Constitution is vague, and it is left to the Court to impose some meaning and consistency on its provisions.

Are the Elected Branches Democratic?

The argument that the Court is undemocratic is also based on the comparative premise that the other branches of government are democratic. Whatever the nondemocratic elements of the rest of government, the Court is clearly the least democratic branch. It is the most removed from the people and the most insulated from the other branches of government. At the outset of the framing of the Constitution, the differences were more of degree than of kind.

A look at the handiwork of the framers reveals that they did not trust democracy. The president was to be elected, not by the people, but by elite electors. Those electors were not bound by the popular vote. Senators would be elected by state legislatures as a concession to federalism. Only members of the House would be elected by the people. Thus, half of one of the three branches of government could be directly elected by the people. "By the people" meant white males who owned property—only they could exercise suffrage. The Constitution hardly established a democracy.

Changes made the elected branches more democratic. Over time, the differences between the elected branches and the judiciary have become more striking. Substantive constitutional amendments extended suffrage to freed slaves, women, and 18–21 year olds. Procedural amendments changed the nature of presidential and senatorial elections to give the voters more influence. Though the electoral college remains in force, electors normally follow the popular vote (although in 2000, Al Gore received more popular votes than George W. Bush, who received a majority in the electoral college). The Constitution did not and does not prescribe a pure democracy. Rather, it is a republican form of government in which political power is diffused among the branches and levels of government that are dependent on each other and accountable to the people (O'Brien 1997, 5).

The argument of those who advocate judicial restraint due to democratic theory is predicated on the belief that the other branches of government are democratic and, thus, legitimate. This requires closer examination. Many critics claim that Congress does not represent the people. Instead, it represents well-heeled groups who can afford access to its members, which has led to a transformation of legislative power: Congress is no longer a deliberative representative body, but has become a conduit for a series of deals between interest groups. Given the power of such groups, few statutes have the consent of the majority, and that undermines democratic concerns (Posner 1997, 184). Congressional committee members band together with interest groups and executive agencies to form cohesive, long-standing subgovernments, often referred to as iron triangles or issue networks (Heclo 1978). These networks of influence dominate policy in their respective areas. Only the president can claim to speak for a national constituency, but he is constrained by a system that renders him ineffective and just another supplicant, particularly in the domestic realm (Miller 1982a, 171).

In general, the rise of "government by judiciary" has been accompanied by the decline of congressional responsibility. Years of public disappointment with Congress have increased reliance on the judicial branch. (Hickok and McDowell 1993, 197). The proliferation of legislation and the delegation of rulemaking to bureaucrats raise "profound questions of how our public policy is actually formulated" (Aldisert 1997, 284). Perhaps most troubling is the construction of vague legislation to avoid political problems, leaving it to the courts to provide the meaning of the legislation, the essence of policymaking. A closer look at the process reveals how that happens. Legislation is written in large part by congressional staff, raising questions about whether policy was derived from elected representatives or from their appointed specialists. The legislation that passes Congress is often couched in generalities and vague language to enable it to survive the hurdles of the process, such as committees, floor debate, and the president's veto. That language has to be translated by someone else. It is often left to the courts and the bureaucrats to interpret and implement the provisions. The policymaking opportunities for the courts thus increase, and the judiciary and bureaucracy end up with the awesome power of interpreting legislation (Hickok and McDowell 1993, 213). Not coincidentally, the judges and bureaucrats are unelected.

Both activists and restraintists believe that it would be better if expert agencies and elected legislatures did the work. What happens, though, if the elected branches fail to measure up to the requirements of the Constitution (Justice 1997b, 310)? What if they become captives of organized interests? Activists are willing to utilize the courts as a policymaker to correct for the shortcomings of the other branches. Restraintists hope the self-correcting mechanisms built into the system will redress the problems; they may be overly optimistic.

As another layer is unpeeled, the picture looks even worse. Elections, through their accountability and responsibility, are supposed to confer legitimacy to govern. However, they may be no more than symbolic exercises, what H. L. Mencken called "carnivals of buncombe." The president is elected by barely half the eligible voters, and not every American is eligible to vote. In a close election, the president may get about 20 percent of the vote of persons eighteen years of age or older. In off-year elections, barely a third of the eligible voters bother to go to the polls. This reduces the influence of democracy to mere symbols. The blame may not lie entirely with an apathetic public. Elections tend to be issueless, hardly inspiring voters or creating meaningful dialogue on public policy questions. The weakness of the two political parties means that campaigns often become personality contests.

The influence of incumbency, whereby more than 90 percent of the members of the House of Representatives are reelected, limits notions of democratic accountability. Congressional scholars have long observed that members pursue constituency service and credit claiming, putting aside coherent policymaking in favor of activities geared toward reelection (Mayhew 1974). This has so frustrated some members of the public that a grassroots movement has tried to pass term limits so that incumbents would be limited by law to a prespecified number of terms. Of course, in a sense, there are term limits because in each and every election voters are free to vote the incumbent out of office. The difficulty of doing so, however, is so apparent that groups have taken the extraordinary step of imposing limits on the number of times an individual can run for reelection.[2]

The Court has to be pragmatic and pay some attention to public opinion and to the other branches, which are tied to the electorate. As de Tocqueville noted, the power of the Supreme Court is "enormous but it is the power of public opinion. They are all-powerful as long as the people respect the law; but they would be impotent against popular neglect or contempt of the law." Federal judges, he wrote, "must be statesmen, wise to discern the signs of the times, not afraid to brave the obstacles that can be subdued, nor slow to turn away from the current when it threatens to sweep them off" (Fisher 1988, 12).

The Practical Realities of American Politics

The problems in the American political system have created a policy vacuum that the judiciary often tries to fill. Judge Jose Cabranes argues that "As our politics have collapsed or proved unwieldy—the parties, the Congress, the post Roosevelt presidency are widely believed to be in disarray—our least democratic branch has become the chief mechanism for serving democratic ends" (O'Brien 1997, 277). The Supreme Court, in particular, winds up dealing with the difficult and controversial issues that seem to paralyze the elected branches.

According to Ronald Downing (1970), the judiciary has become the principal forum for resolving political issues by default. This is due, in no small part, to the abdication of the legislative and executive branches. Many feel that Congress does not have the ability or the will to govern and that the president is too weak. According to Miller (1982a, 185–186), there is little prospect that those two branches will be reformed to permit them to deal with the problems of society. He claims that the courts cannot save the country, but "they may be able to buy time until the elected branches can get their respective acts together."

The inability to make policy, or the lack of will to do so, has not stopped presidents or members of Congress from criticizing the Court or mounting what they know will be a visible symbolic campaign to pass a constitutional amendment to overturn a Supreme Court decision. There is a certain irony going on here: Members of Congress complain about judicial activism, but they contribute to its growth by abdicating their responsibilities or by passing statutes that are vague, are patently unconstitutional, or broadly expand standing to give groups access to the courts (Bamberger 2000).

The seemingly constant existence of divided government, having a president of one party and a Congress of the opposition party, has increased reliance on the judiciary. The gridlock that marks divided government often means that presidential initiatives are bottled up in Congress. Presidents may elect to try to use the courts to achieve their policy goals.

The greater use of the courts seems to be encouraged by the elected branches, at least implicitly (McKeever 1993, 21). The Supreme Court becomes a useful player as Congress tries to avoid many contentiousness issues. The Court can make decisions free of the constraints imposed on elected politicians. Congress leaves the details of statutory schemes for the Court to work out, thus allowing legislators to avoid controversial issues and enhance their prospects for reelection. Congress can embroil the Court in disputes whenever it is convenient. By refusing to act, Congress and the president may create a policy vacuum. Sometimes the Court is reluctant to step into the breach and address the issue. On other occasions, the Court has been all too happy to get involved.

In the end, the Court is frequently accused of usurping the prerogatives of the elected branches often by the very policymakers who pushed or enticed the Court into that position (McKeever 1993, 273). The Court may deflect heat from the elected branches of government. John Hart Ely referred to this phenomenon in reference to the abortion decisions when he wrote, "The sighs of relief as this particular albatross was cut from the legislative and executive necks seemed to me audible" (McKeever 1993, 22). Chief Justice Rehnquist believes that if the Court would stay away from such controversial issues, the elected branches would be forced to deal with them.

A Pluralist Role for the Supreme Court

Concerns for democratic values are mitigated to a degree by the fact that our form of government more approximates a pluralist model than a democratic one. If that is the case, then perhaps a different standard should govern the evaluation of the Court as a policymaker. The Madisonian system, framed in *The Federalist* 10, holds that the sphere of governmental authority needs to be spread out to prevent the concentration of power. In the pluralist system, power is divided among the legislative, executive, and judicial branches, as well as among the national, state, and local levels. It is a government of multiple access points. The converse is, however, that there are multiple veto points as well. To get policy enacted, it must go through the legislative and executive branches and survive judicial scrutiny. After its enactment, the policy must be implemented. There are a number of opportunities to kill or emasculate possible initiatives.

Pluralism means that interest groups have access and power. Indeed, interest groups can be seen as bridges across the divide of separated powers and federalism. They can create a uniform presence at the state and national level and before each of the branches of government. As a result, Theodore Lowi (1979) and Grant McConnell (1966), among others, say that there are no public interest or national values, just a series of parochial values pushed by interest groups. Theorists believe pluralism is not a self-correcting mechanism. They contend that our form of pluralism has created a vacuum of moral and authoritative leadership, which has been filled by the Court (Miller 1982a, 176–178). Within the classic pluralist model, courts are seen as another outlet for the redress of grievances.

The Supreme Court became an important actor in the pluralist system when it adopted the double standard for judicial decisionmaking. In economic issues, the Court would exercise judicial restraint and defer to the elected branches of government. In cases involving the rights of "insular minorities," the Court would exercise judicial activism. In a series of decisions that reached a climax in *Brown v. Board of Education* and *Baker v. Carr* (1963), the Court presented itself as a forum for groups that were excluded from the elected branches of government. Civil rights proponents knew that the legislation they favored had virtually no chance of surviving Senate filibusters. They welcomed the opportunity to use the Supreme Court. The Court also became the province for issues that were not suitable or appropriate for the elected branches (Pacelle 1991, 140–141). Civil liberties issues—most notably the protection of religious minorities, unpopular groups such as Communists, Nazis, and the Ku Klux Klan and criminal defendants—would stand little chance of a fair hearing before elected officials. While one might not shed any tears if some of these groups had their rights diminished, civil libertarians would argue that restrictions on the rights of those groups could create the environment for broader restrictions on the rights and liberties of everyone else.

Some believe that the Court serves a vital function when it opens its doors to groups that are disenfranchised in the other branches. Then, those groups can have a stake in society. The Court may be siphoning off discontent by providing a forum for groups without any other recourse. Civil rights was the classic example. The justices exercised judicial activism to open the schools, voting booths, the workplace, and the housing market to African Americans. The long-term goal was to open the political process for fuller participation. The Court must not only decide what the government can and cannot do, but determine what would be necessary to preserve democracy (McKeever 1993, 274–275). Thus, an undemocratic institution might actually be protecting and expanding democracy.

Charles Epp (1998, 4–5) claims the undemocratic nature of judicial decisionmaking is overstated. In the areas of civil rights and civil liberties, Epp maintains that Supreme Court policymaking is not strictly a top-down creation of the justices; rather, the rights revolution was largely a function of a bottom-up phenomenon. "The rights revolution depended on widespread support made possible by the democratization of access to the judiciary." In his view, "the meaning of 'democracy' is thus complex and nuanced" (5).

The process of long-term doctrinal development and policymaking in civil rights and individual liberties was created by the justices and litigants who respond to the decisions of the Court and prepare the next round of litigation. Epp (1998, 67–70) believes there is a democratic element to the process: Broadly based groups with financial and litigation help from other groups have created an external support structure that has fueled the process of policymaking. Thus, the Supreme Court has helped to create and nourish legal mobilization. The other branches of government have aided the prospects for legal mobilization and helped the support structure flourish. Congress has aided the process by passing legislation that makes it easier to use the courts for the redress of grievances. Congress created the Legal Services Commission to help the poor and passed civil rights legislation to make it easier to sue. The Department of Justice, through the Solicitor General, who argues cases for the U.S. government, has acted as an *amicus curiae*[3] and as a party to protect the rights of groups and individuals (Epp 1998, 58–63). The assistance of the elected branches suggests a democratic element to the construction and maintenance of rights.

Pluralism has a number of practical consequences that could alter democratic perspectives on the appropriate role of the Court. As noted, groups have great influence in American politics. However, E. E. Schattschneider (1975) noted that because of interest groups, "the heavenly chorus sings with a strong upper class accent." The haves benefit from this arrangement, while the have-nots continue to struggle for some institutional recognition. Political scientists contend that Congress makes much of its policy in small subgovernments that operate with relative invisibility and have complete control over their issue areas. Those subgovernments do not have to compete with each other for resources or programs.

Pluralism and subgovernments affect the government's ability to plan or make the hard choices to balance the federal budget. It is difficult for policymakers in the elected branches to develop coherent, broadly based initiatives to deal with the nation's problems. If these subgovernments can effectively control their respective areas, that means there are dozens of issues that cannot be factored into governmental planning.

If, as Lowi (1979) claims, American government is incapable of planning and pluralism means that broad-range policies are impossible, activists would argue that the Court should step into the vacuum. As Judge William Wayne Justice (1997b, 311), an avowed judicial activist, argued, "If the law makes empty promises of justice and courts stand by impotently watching constitutional violations persist without taking action to correct them, then we do not fulfill the promises of equal protection and due process." Those who are not troubled by the undemocratic nature of the Court believe that the political system has some serious defects, the most notable of which is the absence of any institution that regularly deals with fundamental political and moral problems. The judiciary is seen as best suited to deal with human rights issues precisely because it is undemocratic (McKeever 1993, 41–42).

Rights and Liberties: The Province of the Supreme Court

De Tocqueville feared that democracy could degenerate into a tyranny of the majority over minorities. The Court can be a bulwark to protect the latter from the former. This has not been a traditional role of the Court. Rather, it was adopted by the Court in the wake of controversy over the New Deal. Today, some analysts and justices consider it to be the ultimate justification for having unelected justices and letting them make policies.

Even many of those who believe that democratic values and principles should dominate the Court's concerns and that the judiciary should exercise restraint concede that there are some issues that call for increased judicial activism. In the twentieth century, the Court took for itself the power to protect civil rights and individual liberties. Since the Court adopted the role of the protector of insular minorities, it has frequently been in conflict with majority sentiment (O'Brien 1997, 4).

In footnote four of his *United States v. Carolene Products* opinion, Justice Stone urged the Court to monitor and overturn laws that disadvantaged individuals and groups who lacked access to the representative process. His justification for this activism was the very undemocratic nature of the Court that troubles many analysts. Stone's so-called manifesto in a footnote is consistent with Hamilton's view that certain provisions are removed from majoritarian authority (Justice 1997a, 159).

Situational judicial activism is at the heart of Stone's preferred position doctrine. Michael Perry (1982) would preclude the use of judicial review in those areas in which the other branches are competent, most notably economic issues. However, in areas such as civil liberties, he claims the judiciary has developed expertise that is unmatched and nonexistent in the rest of the political system. Thus, the Court would be free to act aggressively in protecting those rights.

Many of these rights are vested in the Bill of Rights, which was designed to be countermajoritarian and showed that the framers intended the Court to have a special role in the protection of individual rights. In this respect, the Constitution is not entirely democratic (Wallace 1997, 163). Some provisions of the Bill of Rights invite the courts to develop and apply their notions of good social policy (such as the Eighth Amendment, because notions of cruel and unusual punishment change with the times) (McKeever 1993, 275–276). Increasingly, the appropriate role of the courts is being viewed as making the difficult decisions in a detached and fair way and standing as a guardian against the potential tyranny of the majority.

Judicial activism is least controversial when justices act to preserve democratic principles and power. Primarily, the Court needs to follow egalitarian principles and keep open the channels of a representative political process, the area in which it is the weakest. When the Court makes decisions that ensure voting rights, keep access to government open, and preserve the right to debate political issues, it is fulfilling an important objective and is justified in using judicial review. Even restraintists concede this point.

Under our system, the people are sovereign, and they expressed their will in a written Constitution. Majority rule is the dominant concept, but sometimes majorities follow a dangerous path. The document set up the basic rules of the government, and the Court has to enforce them. Relatedly, the argument is offered that the Constitution established a limited government and if the elected branches ignore those limits, then it is appropriate for the justices to step in and review their handiwork. Insistence on democratic principles leads to aggressive Court policymaking; other issues should lead to judicial restraint (Goldstein 1995, 284–292).

Some would say that the debate over the proper role of the Court in a democracy is the product of a bygone era. The Supreme Court has entrenched itself as a policymaker in civil rights and individual liberties over the last sixty years and should continue this role. The Court has also expanded its power as a function of the weakness of the other branches and their lack of will, particularly in the areas of civil rights and individual liberties.

Civil liberties generally refer to protections against governmental intrusion and normally require the Court to enjoin the government from committing some act that would violate those liberties. Civil rights, on the other hand, require the government to take positive steps to ensure equal protection of the law. Many of these decisions, particularly the remedies for violation of civil rights, have been more controversial. To remedy racial discrimination in the schools, the Supreme Court ordered massive busing. To remedy racial discrimination in employment and university admissions, the Court permitted affirmative action. The use of broad remedies is judicial activism and places the Court into a difficult political position. In addition, it often leads the Court into direct conflict with the elected branches of government.

Many scholars claim these remedies represent the modern brand of judicial activism that is marked by less deference to elected decisionmakers and majoritarian sentiments. This modern judicial activism is reflected in the power to revise the Constitution by interpretation. Many controversial decisions were issued by the Warren Court, but it was the Burger Court that recognized busing and affirmative action and created reproductive rights. Indeed, many analysts liked the results of these decisions, but took exception to the manner in which they were made. The activist Supreme Court after *Brown* was accused of legislating from the bench and creating constitutional rights where none existed.

Democratic Concerns Revisited

There has been a renewed interest in the democratic controversy in the last decade. The Warren Court took the initiative in a number of areas and took the authority for decisionmaking away from state and local governments. The Court did this through decisions such as *Brown*, which imposed some measure of federal control over education (a traditional state function) and by incorporating the Bill of Rights. Such decisions served to supplant the influence of elected government at the level in which most authoritative policy decisions were made (McKeever 1993, 274). In addition, these decisions removed the consideration of some issues from democratic decisionmakers and placed power in the hands of unelected judges.

There have been reversals of some of these patterns during the tenure of Chief Justice Rehnquist, in hopes of bringing the judiciary more in line with democratic theory. A majority has tried to turn the locus of power back to state and local governments (McKeever 1993, 275). The Rehnquist Court has tried to redefine its institutional role. A number of the current justices advocate a rejection of the double standard. They support judicial restraint and deference to the elected branches regardless of the issue. They argue that the Court should adopt a secondary role, filling in gaps, but not taking the lead in policymaking.

The "new" philosophy, which represents a return to past doctrines, advocates attention to the original intent of the framers of the Constitution and a stricter construction of the document. In practical terms, these justices desire to balance individual rights and competing social interests on a more equal footing than the preferred position doctrine would advocate. This theory is complemented by an increased willingness to defer to the elected branches in civil liberties and civil rights, thus rejecting the twentieth-century liberalism that has guided Court decisions and policymaking in these areas (Smith 1985).

Rehnquist has long considered the Court to be at fault in triggering many of the problems identified here. Judicial activism, particularly during the Warren Court, gave the elected branches of government the opportunity to dodge the contentious issues of the day. Congress got used to allowing the Court to take the heat for the controversies of the day. Rehnquist concedes that the elected branches often left a vacuum when it came to important public policy issues. But the Court was too anxious to step into this breach, relieving the elected branches of their democratic responsibilities. Rehnquist argued that had the Court bided its time and not rushed in, Congress would have been forced to confront the issues.[4] The initial results tend to confirm his suspicions. As the Court retreated from making public policy, a Democratic Congress in the 1980s did indeed pass civil rights and voting rights legislation (Cheney 1998, 35–38). Some would argue that the election of a Republican Congress in the 1990s removed this safety net.

In the long term, such policies might signal a new role for the Supreme Court, one that would advocate judicial restraint and deference to other agencies of government, the core of traditional normative values. Most fundamentally, these changes have implications for the treatment of individual rights and liberties, the dominant staple of the Court's agenda. Civil liberties issues may receive the same type of balancing tests the Court has used in economic issues. The Court would be less directly involved in the fundamental construction of policy than the Warren Court.

The Rehnquist Court has made it more difficult for litigants. A majority amended Supreme Court Rule 39, which provided the poor access to the courts, to permit the Court to deny "frivolous or malicious" filings. Former Justice Thurgood Marshall penned the most pointed dissent, claiming that the Court's once great tradition would now be: "All men and women are entitled to their day in Court only if they have the *means* and the *money.*" Though the practical effects of the amended Rule 39 may be unclear, the symbolic message is testimony to the changes in the Court's perspective. The Court also tightened restrictions on civil rights suits.

These concurrent trends suggest that the Court may be undergoing an institutional transformation that would be similar (if philosophically opposed) to the changes wrought in the wake of footnote four in *Carolene Products*. Changing the role of the Court would have significant implications for notions of pluralism. Since 1937, insular minorities and unpopular groups have had a forum in the Supreme Court. If this avenue is foreclosed, it might mean the disenfranchisement of a number of groups. One remaining point of access would be the state courts, which might create a patchwork of protections that would vary from state to state or region to region—a stark contrast to the Warren Court's attempts to standardize the law through the incorporation of the Bill of Rights to the states and an expansive interpretation of the Fourteenth Amendment.

Conclusion

Chief Justice Rehnquist (1997, 144–145) maintains that judicial review must be used sparingly and that the use of this power must be tied to the language of the Constitution. Failing to embrace this, Rehnquist claims, leads to judges who are not "the keepers of the covenant" but a "roving commission to second guess Congress, state legislatures, and state and federal administrative officers concerning what is best for the country."[5] This is the classic statement of the democratic dilemma: unelected justices substituting their judgment for those of the duly elected representatives.

Traditional judicial review was controversial, of course, but the Court tried to maintain democratic credentials when it was being used. Thus, it was broadly acceptable. Judicial review was deemed acceptable only because justices enforced the will of the framers (Wallace 1997, 165). In civil rights and individual liberties, however, proponents of judicial activism could echo the question posed by Justice Thurgood Marshall: How can the Constitution and the framers be determinative when women and blacks were denied any rights?

Modern judicial review has become more controversial because there is a perception that the justices are no longer tethered to the Constitution or the neutral principles to justify their decisions. Rather, they are seen as deliberate policy-makers who attempt to legislate from the bench.

Most analysts and justices agree that when the elected branches clearly cross the line, judicial activism is justified, even mandated. In addition, when the ends preserve the democratic process, judicial activism is justified. The question of whether an elected official crossed the lines tests one's belief in judicial restraint (Wallace 1997, 165). It is, in effect, the million-dollar question for justices.

How seriously should the democratic constraint on judicial policymaking be taken? Certainly, justices are unelected and thus not accountable to the citizens. On the other hand, many of the democratic mechanisms have been perverted to some degree, suggesting that the differences between the elected and unelected branches have blurred.

Perhaps the ultimate justification for judicial activism is the undemocratic nature of the judiciary. Governmental institutions have evolved to the point where the responsibility for the protection of individual rights is placed in the hands of an unelected judiciary. Only the Court is insulated from the ebb and flow of public opinion. This provides the Court with the opportunity to protect the rights of minorities. With members of Congress and the president having to face the voters, it is perhaps wishful thinking to hope that they would stand up for the rights of unpopular minorities.

In stating his Court's opposition to the preferred position doctrine, Chief Justice Rehnquist argued that the Court should take great pains to avoid active policymaking. In particular, the Court should avoid the controversial issues that prove its institutional weaknesses, violate democratic principles, test its capacity, and risk its very legitimacy. In Rehnquist's view, if the Court has the will and the strength to avoid these difficult issues, the elected branches will have to step into the vacuum. That would save the Court and put decisionmaking in the hands that the framers intended.

Democratic principles are not enough of an argument to counteract judicial activism in all circumstances. In fact, it is the notion of majority rule and democracy that is the single most persuasive argument for situational judicial activism. The Court needs to stand up for minority rights because no one else has the institutional position to do so. However, when the Supreme Court tries to fashion broad-scale remedies to correct perceived abuses, it invites a number of risks and tests its normative and empirical limits. In the next two chapters, the institutional and capacity dimensions of the dilemma will be assessed.

Notes

1. Multiple veto points refers to the fact that although the American political system offers a number of points of access for groups and individuals seeking to enact a policy proposal (the executive, legislative, and judicial branches as well as state and local branches), policy initiatives must nevertheless survive all those points of access. Opponents have many opportunities to defeat a proposed policy by blocking it in committee or one house of Congress, by a presidential veto, in the formulation of bureaucratic rules, in implementation, or in the courts.

2. The Supreme Court declared term limits unconstitutional in *U.S. Term Limits, Inc. v. Thornton* 514 US 779 (1995). To pass term limits would require a constitutional amendment.

3. The *amicus curiae*, or friend of the court, brief allows groups who are not parties to the case to participate and have the opportunity to tell the Court how they will be affected by the decision.

4. This is one of the central arguments that Rosenberg (1991) makes. Those seeking policy goals would be advised to go through Congress, rather than the courts. Rosenberg argues that not only did the Court not achieve its goals in *Brown*, but it actually left civil rights in a worse situation than if it had done nothing and forced the other branches to act.

5. The evidence is mixed as to whether the Court practices what the chief justice preaches. The Court has declared many federal laws, but very few state laws, unconstitutional.

4

The Institutional Dimension of the Dilemma: Constitutional and Self-Imposed Limitations

INSTITUTIONAL CONCERNS focus on the power and, more precisely, the limits on the power of the judicial branch. There are significant limitations on the ability of the Supreme Court to make public policy in a coherent fashion. Such limits might suggest that the Court should work cautiously and avoid making sweeping policy pronouncements. Rather, the Court should operate at the margins, filling in gaps and letting the elected branches take the lead in policymaking because they have the institutional power to do so. The limitations that the rules of the Supreme Court impose on the justices are strong arguments for judicial restraint. But can the Court overcome these constraints to take part in policymaking? Consider two examples:

Despite the fact that much of the rest of the world was at war, the attack on the naval base at Pearl Harbor caught the United States by surprise. At the time, the American military was woefully underprepared. The early morning attack was labeled an act of cowardice by President Franklin Roosevelt. The Allied military was battling German, Italian, and Japanese forces. On the home front, Italian Americans and German Americans were not considered threats or necessarily open to subversive activities. According to the government, though, the same could not be said of Japanese Americans. The government targeted Japanese Americans living on the West Coast and relocated them to the American equivalent of concentration camps. Fred Korematsu challenged the detention order and placed the Supreme Court in the middle of a conflict. Many of the justices viewed the relocation order with great suspicion, but there were constraints on their ability to review the government's policy. It was wartime, and the nine justices isolated in Washington were in little position to second-guess those who had to make strategic military decisions or to challenge the government in military or foreign affairs. As a result, the Court had to give its stamp of approval to the relocation policy. Some of the justices explained that they felt compelled to defer to the political branches under these circumstances.[1]

The decision to permit the detention of Japanese Americans in *Korematsu v. United States* (1944) is universally regarded as one of the darkest moments in Supreme Court history. The decision pointed out the weaknesses that affect the Supreme Court and the limits on the justices in certain circumstances. The Court lacks the institutional power to combat the elected branches in times of war.

The Vietnam War was the first war televised into American homes. Though it became increasingly unpopular, Presidents Johnson and Nixon did not scale back the war effort in the face of that opposition. During the 1960s, the Supreme Court had proven itself to be amenable to broad extensions of constitutional rights. As a consequence, there were a number of attempts to see if the Supreme Court would find the Vietnam War unconstitutional. That issue was indirectly before the Court in *Schlesinger v. Reservists Committee to Stop the War* (1974).[2] Although three justices were willing to consider the bigger issue of the war's constitutionality within the context of this case, a majority held that the litigants lacked standing. They ruled that such issues fell under the "political questions doctrine," meaning that they should be addressed by the elected branches of government, not the courts (Fisher 1988, 89; Epstein and Walker 1998a, 108). There were practical reasons to avoid confronting the issue. What if the Court ultimately declared the war unconstitutional? Most likely, Congress and the president would have ignored the decision, costing the Court its legitimacy.

These examples, both occurring during times of military action, point out some of the institutional constraints that the Supreme Court faces. The Court has some inherent weaknesses that limit its ability to make public policy under the best of circumstances. In addition, the Court's rules may limit the types of issues or questions that it can address. Are such institutional limitations on the Court strong enough to suggest that the justices should impose judicial restraint on their decisionmaking?

The Court is a peculiar institution for a policymaker. In *The Federalist* 81, Alexander Hamilton discussed the comparative weaknesses of the judiciary. He claimed the danger of judicial encroachment on legislative power was a "phantom" concern. The institutional limitations on the Supreme Court are very clear from the Constitution, which is organized around two principles: separation of powers and checks and balances. In dividing power among the three branches, the judiciary truly appeared to be the least dangerous branch. In devising checks and balances, the Supreme Court received the fewest resources to protect itself from the other branches. In fact, it had to create its own power through judicial review.

This chapter starts with the constitutional limitations on the Supreme Court, then turns to the limitations on the Court's power: the process, jurisdiction, justiciability, and checks and balances. How the Court has overcome some of these constraints to exercise power and make public policy is considered briefly.

The Limits of the Judicial Branch

The Constitutional Limits

Article I of the Constitution lists seventeen specific powers for the legislative branch and contains an open-ended implied powers clause that grants Congress the authority to take action that is necessary and proper to carry out its enumerated powers. The framers clearly intended for Congress to be the central power in the governmental structure. Article II gives the president far less power, but includes authority to veto legislation, appointment power shared with Congress, and the prerogatives attendant to being commander in chief. In addition, the president is vested with executive power and he shall "take care" that the laws be faithfully executed.[3] The fact that the chief executive and the vice president would be the only individuals elected nationally provided a potential for executive power that was not lost on the framers.

By contrast, Article III provided the Supreme Court with a reservoir of power and authority that appeared to be an inch deep and not very wide. Article III limits the Court's original jurisdiction to cases involving ambassadors, public ministers, and consuls. The Court's appellate jurisdiction is controlled by Congress. The brevity and vagueness of Article III forced Congress and the Court to fill in the details. As with Article II, dealing with the executive branch, the vagueness would later become a source of significant power; but, at the time, there was more concern that the Court would have little to do.

Even if the Supreme Court was to carve out some sphere of power for itself, there would be significant limitations. Any Court decision has to be enforced, but enforcement power is the province of the president and the executive branch. Thus, the Court is at their mercy. If the president does not like the decision, he does not have to enforce it. Indeed, history books report that Andrew Jackson, upset at the *Worcester v. Georgia* (1832) decision, growled that "John Marshall made his decision, now let him enforce it." There was concern that Dwight Eisenhower would not back the *Brown* decision when the Southern states resisted. Ultimately, though quite reluctantly, Eisenhower sent troops to Little Rock to support the decision.

What if the Court's decision requires active policy intervention and the allocation of resources to help carry out the directives? If the courts determine that prisons are overcrowded or schools are substandard, will the legislature, which has the taxing and spending power, be willing to raise and spend money to correct the problem? It took a decade before serious legislative support for the *Brown* decision was provided. Title VI of the Civil Rights Act of 1964 empowered the government to cut off federal funds to school districts that did not comply with the desegregation directive (Halpern 1995, 30–59).

The bottom line is the adage "the Court lacks the sword and the purse"—it lacks the ability to enforce its decisions and the power over the resources to do so. This places a limitation on the justices. If they stray too far from the acceptable boundaries set by Congress or the president, they risk a negative response from the branches with the real power. If the Court can safely be ignored by the other branches and the public, the cost is its institutional legitimacy.

Further suggesting the Court's inherent institutional weaknesses are the limited checks that the Court holds over the other branches. The most significant check, judicial review, was notable by its absence from the Constitution. That power was not created until Chief Justice John Marshall made his decision in *Marbury v. Madison* in 1803. However, the records of the Constitutional Convention have led many scholars to conclude that the framers intended to provide judicial review to the Court. They claim the debates show that members of the convention appeared to assume the Court would exercise this power (Witt 1981, 3). Still, it is odd that this check was not mentioned in the document. Judicial review is a major resource, to be sure, but the Court does not use it that often (about 150 times in the 1803–2000 period) (Baum 2001, 195), suggesting that the threat is enough. The limited use of judicial review also suggests that the Court's policymaking power must be derived from other sources.

The Supreme Court appeared to be an afterthought for the framers. As a consequence of the weaknesses of the institution, being a justice of the Supreme Court was not considered a plum appointment. Only three of the six justices were present on the first day of the Court's opening session in 1789. The justices adjourned a scant nine days later. That was much longer than the second term, 1790, which lasted two days. No cases were decided by the Court in 1791 or 1792. A number of nominees refused their appointments, preferring to stay in the state legislature. Justices left the Supreme Court for positions such as governor of New York and state court judges. The first chief justice, John Jay, left the Court because it lacked the "energy, weight, and dignity" to contribute to national affairs (Witt 1981, 7). Perhaps the clearest symbol of its weakness was the fact that when the new capital was being built, the Court was overlooked and no chambers were provided for the justices. Rather, the Court ended up in "an undignified committee room . . . beneath the House Chamber" (Schwartz 1993, 16).

Limitations on the Authority of the Supreme Court

The limitations on judicial power seem to suggest that the Court should exercise judicial restraint to avoid extending its power beyond its boundaries. Those limitations take a variety of forms: Some are attendant to the judicial process; others include jurisdiction, justiciability, and checks and balances. Many of those constraints are spelled out in Article III; others are implied. Table 4.1 lists the institutional limitations on the Court and the potential for judicial power.

Judicial procedures limit the Court's ability to make public policy. First, without the "sword and the purse," the Court cannot assume that its decisions will be carried

TABLE 4.1 Constraints on the Supreme Court and Opportunities for Power

Limitations on Judicial Power	Potential of Judicial Power
Process	Judicial review
Jurisdiction	Constitutional interpretation
Justiciability	Flexibility of rules of access
Checks and balances	Institutional legitimacy

Source: Richard Pacelle.

out. More broadly, the Court is a passive institution, a problem for a policymaker. The Court does not have the ability to determine its own agenda; rather, it must wait for cases to arrive. Congress and the president are under no such constraints. This places limits on the Court that do not encumber the elected branches, implying that the Court is not the appropriate place for addressing public policy issues.

Additionally, the Court makes policy by deciding individual cases, but it is difficult to make coherent public policy on a case-by-case basis. The appropriate case for a decision that has far-ranging consequences may not be on the docket. The Court has to choose between the two litigants in the particular cases, but its decision has implications for all similar cases. Students of the Court often contend that these limitations should be signals to the justices that they should exhibit restraint (Horowitz 1977)—manifested in narrow decisions, upholding precedent, and limited judicial legislating. These perceived weaknesses of the Court do not sway judicial activists. They tend to favor broader review and sweeping remedies (Wolfe 1997, 4). Activists tend to construct broadly based decisions and precedents and would not let institutional constraints interfere with their policy goals. Questions about the effects of these constraints on the Court as a policymaker involve concerns with judicial capacity and are the subject of Chapter 5.

The rules that govern the judicial process are tied to notions of jurisdiction and justiciability. The Supreme Court must have the jurisdiction or authority to decide a particular case. The Court's appellate jurisdiction is largely controlled by Congress, which holds this potential check over the Court. Over the last half-century, members of Congress have introduced dozens of proposals to limit the Court's jurisdiction. If Congress does not like a particular decision, it can rescind the Court's authority to hear those types of cases.

Article III limits the Supreme Court to deciding cases and controversies. Justiciability refers to the question of whether judges should hear a particular case or refrain from accepting it. In essence, that means that a case must be appropriate or suitable for a court (Epstein and Walker 1998a, 58). The rules limit what the judiciary can and cannot do and limit the kinds of disputes the courts can consider. The most basic constraint on the Court is that it must wait for a suitable case or controversy to arise. It cannot just reach out and consider hypothetical issues. Rather, a case with two adversarial parties must be properly before the justices.

Finally, the other branches of government hold checks and balances over the Supreme Court that can limit its power and authority. Of the four forms of imposed limitations—the judicial process, jurisdiction, justiciability, and checks and balances—two are internal to the Court (process and justiciability) and two are external (jurisdiction and checks and balances). The internal limitations ask the Court to impose restraint on itself. External constraints are imposed by outside actors and may be triggered by judicial activism.

Jurisdiction

A potential constraint on the Supreme Court, jurisdiction refers to the authority of a court to hear and decide cases and is, in large part, externally derived. As David O'Brien (2000, 169) notes, "Jurisdiction is power over access to justice and the exercise of judicial review." The Court's jurisdiction comes from three sources: Article III of the Constitution, congressional legislation concerning appellate jurisdiction, and the Court's interpretation of its own power and authority. The potential fragility of the Court's jurisdiction is an argument for judicial restraint. If the Court exhibits restraint, it will not antagonize Congress. If the Court exercises too much activism, it risks incurring the ire of Congress, which may threaten or repeal some of its jurisdiction and cost the Court some of its legitimacy.

Article III of the Constitution gives the Supreme Court very limited original jurisdiction. The term *original* means that the case starts in that particular court. Almost every case that gets to the Supreme Court begins in trial courts of original jurisdiction. However, cases involving ambassadors, ministers, and consuls begin in the Supreme Court because of the desire to avoid disrespecting officials from other nations by making them traverse the entire judicial process. One other class of cases that would begin in the Supreme Court are those involving disputes between two states, often border disputes. Original jurisdiction cases make up a very small fraction of the Court's docket and, substantively, do not constitute very significant issues.

The remainder of the Court's jurisdiction is referred to as appellate. Appellate jurisdiction means that the Supreme Court would review cases after a lower court had made the original judgment. The Supreme Court's most important cases arrive after one, two, or in some instances, three courts have decided the facts and reviewed the legal issues. The problem for the justices is that the Court's appellate jurisdiction is controlled by Congress.

Article III holds that the Court has appellate jurisdiction "with such Exceptions, and under such Regulation as the Congress shall make." The Exceptions Clause gives Congress some authority to alter the Court's jurisdiction. How extensive is that power? Congress has occasionally altered the Supreme Court's jurisdiction, but many of these changes have been done in a neutral fashion to assist the Court in handling its growing caseload. Prior to 1925, the Court had to hear every case that was properly brought before it. Because of the Court's burgeoning caseload, Congress gave the Court some control over its agenda by passing an act in 1925 that created the discretionary writ of *certiorari*. Some cases still had to be heard, via a writ of appeal, but most were at the Court's discretion. In 1988, Congress further extended the reach of the writ of certiorari, leaving only a handful of cases that the Supreme Court must hear. In both instances, Congress was responding to requests by the justices that their jurisdiction be altered to provide them with more control (Perry 1991).

In other circumstances, attempts to alter the Court's jurisdiction have been far from neutral and not designed to help the Supreme Court. Often they involved a reaction to a Court decision that members of Congress opposed. Members of Congress have occasionally operated on the notion that if they did not like a decision or a certain doctrinal trend by the Supreme Court, they could simply take away its authority or jurisdiction to hear those kinds of cases. While Congress has not actually stripped specific jurisdiction, it is uncertain whether it could do so and survive constitutional scrutiny. That has not deterred Congress from trying, however.

Many of the most controversial issues of the last half-century have ended up in the Supreme Court. The Court's decisions are bound to provoke a response from those who disapprove of them. A number of decisions have led members of Congress to introduce legislation to limit or deny jurisdiction. In the 1960s, a Congress that reflected public opposition to the Warren Court's criminal procedure decisions tried to remove the Court's ability to hear state cases involving confessions. A decade later, decisions supporting school busing to achieve desegregation prompted a response from Congress seeking to remove the Court's authority to hear such cases or to limit remedial orders. Congress attacked the Court's jurisdiction to hear school prayer cases after the Court placed limits on mandatory prayer in the classroom. The abortion decisions also led to attacks on the Court's jurisdiction (Epstein and Walker 1998a, 88).

None of these efforts succeeded. Some members of Congress, even those who oppose the Court's decisions, have considered it unwise to tamper with jurisdiction. There is a practical reason for this: The membership of the Court may change and create a majority sympathetic to congressional designs. The new Court would lack the authority to pursue the goal Congress sought in the first place. More broadly, there are other considerations at play. It is risky for one branch of government to tamper with the powers of another for two reasons: It creates a precedent for attacking the Court when powerful members of Congress oppose a particular decision, and it undermines respect for the judiciary as an institution. Respect and legitimacy are the Court's ultimate resources.

The Court, of course, could co-opt these threats by exercising restraint or retreating in the face of a congressional threat. Congressional attacks on the Court's jurisdiction do not necessarily need to become law to have a desired effect. In *Watkins v. United States* (1957), the Supreme Court placed limits on the power of the House Un-American Activities Committee to inquire into the political beliefs of alleged Communist sympathizers and their associates. It came as no surprise that Congress reacted immediately and strongly. Not only was this an unpopular decision because it freed alleged Communists, it struck directly at the power of a committee of the House of Representatives. A number of Court-curbing bills were introduced to remove these questions from judicial purview (Powe 2000, 95–98). That legislation was pending when a similar case, *Barenblatt v. United States* (1959), arrived on the Court's docket. One could imagine that Barenblatt's attorney was relatively confident, having a favorable, recent precedent that seemed to be directly on point. Instead, the Court, appearing to bow to congressional pressure, did not restrict HUAC's power to hold Lloyd Barenblatt in contempt when he refused to answer its questions.

The issue of whether Congress could actually restrict the Court's jurisdiction remains open. Right after the Civil War, Congress tried to take away the Court's jurisdiction to hear cases involving *habeas corpus*. The Court acceded, ruling that it did not have the authority to consider the appeal. The Court's decision was based on political expediency and the desire to retain its legitimacy (Pritchett 1984a, 114). The case provides little guidance for the question of whether Congress could attack jurisdiction in specific issue areas.

While Congress has restricted cases addressed by the Court, it has also done the opposite. Congress has created a variety of rights and made it easier for plaintiffs to get into court, thus expanding the Court's jurisdiction. Congress opened the door to more types of litigation and, on more than one occasion, condemned the Court when it took the next logical step.

Justiciability

There are certain rules of access or technical criteria that potential cases must meet in order to be considered justiciable. Article III of the Constitution states that the Court should only decide actual cases and controversies. The parties to the case must be adversaries and have a live dispute. If the dispute is the province of the elected branches, the Court should leave the determination to them. These rules or criteria, however, are flexible and self-imposed and internally based: The justices can decide whether or not to enforce the rules and refuse to take a case or ignore the case's problems (and thus the rules) and decide the issue.

In general, a litigant must have standing to sue in order to proceed with a case. *Standing* is a general term referring to the principle that the Court should not resolve hypothetical questions. At the core of the principle is that the litigant in the case must be injured in order to bring a case forward. In legal terms, the Court is not supposed to decide cases that are not "ripe," that are "moot," or where the parties lack "standing to sue." The Court is not supposed to issue "advisory opinions" or to entertain "political questions."

In addition to being a general concept, standing is also a specific term, dealing with the parties to the case and whether they are properly before the court. Standing is a threshold requirement to get into court, meaning that there has to be an actual case or controversy. The parties involved in the case must demonstrate a real injury in order to use the courts. If an individual lacks a personal interest or stake in the outcome of the case, the Supreme Court should dismiss the petition (O'Brien 2000, 175–178).

As specific concepts, standing, ripeness, and mootness are related. Standing is the present state of the relationship between the two parties to the case. Ripeness is the future state of standing, while mootness is the past state of standing.

The ripeness doctrine means that the Supreme Court will not consider a case unless it is ripe for resolution. The case has to have gone through all the necessary previous channels or the alleged harm in the case has not yet materialized. If someone challenges a law before it has taken effect or before its predicted impact has occurred, the Supreme Court is supposed to dismiss the petition because it is not yet ripe for determination. Ripeness means, in effect, that standing has not yet occurred in the case.

Mootness refers to a situation in which the litigant had standing when the case began in the lower court, but by the time it progressed to the Supreme Court, standing no longer existed. When a case is moot, it means that the matter has been resolved. Thus, the Supreme Court's ultimate decision would have no effect on the parties in the case because the controversy has been settled (Epstein and Walker 1998a, 90–91).

Occasionally, friendly parties might get together to test a law even if they have no disagreement in the case. These are referred to as feigned or collusive cases. If the interests of the party are not adverse, then the motivation for bringing out all the relevant information may be lacking. This is particularly problematic if the constitutionality of a federal law is challenged and both parties want the statute declared null and void (Pritchett 1984a, 158). The Supreme Court is not supposed to decide cases when both parties want the same result and are merely trying to create a test case.

The early Supreme Court created a precedent that justices cannot issue advisory opinions. Secretary of State Thomas Jefferson had asked the Court to render a judgment about a series of questions tied to a treaty between France and the United States. Chief Justice Jay refused to provide an opinion. He told Jefferson that the Court could only decide actual cases and not render opinions on hypothetical cases (O'Brien 2000, 172–174). While the Supreme Court almost invariably declines invitations to render advisory opinions, many state courts have the authority to provide such opinions to the governor or the state legislature.

Finally, the Supreme Court is not supposed to decide "political questions," cases that are the province of the elected branches. The so-called political questions doctrine is tied to the Court's constraints: The Court is supposed to avoid cases in which it lacks the resources to decide or the means to enforce its decisions. On one level, virtually every case before the Court is a political question. However, the Supreme Court is supposed to refuse to decide cases better suited for the political branches because they are inappropriate for judicial resolution. The Court often defines political questions as those that involve disputes within or between the executive and legislative branches (O'Brien 2000, 182–183).

In each of these instances, the Court is supposed to refuse to address the substantive issue because of some defect in the particular case. These problems provide the Court with an excuse to avoid difficult or potentially controversial cases. However, there is nothing automatic about these rules of access. The question of justiciability is largely self-regulated. If there is a potential problem with a case, it takes a majority to refuse to decide that case. If a majority wants to decide the case despite its defects, the case will be accepted and decided on the merits. Thus, the rules of access are tied to notions of judicial activism and restraint.

The strict enforcement of the rules of access is an act of judicial self-restraint. By refusing to accept a case because of the rules of access, the justices do not deal with the issue at hand and adopt a passive role. Because the Court is the arbiter of its own rules, however, it can enforce or ignore the rules (O'Brien 2000, 172). To ignore the rules means that the Court will take cases despite their defects. This would be an example of judicial activism that allows the justices to address a case that might not be appropriately before the Court.

The bottom line is that application of these rules is far from neutral. In general, justices who refuse to enforce the rules of access are willing to open the doors of the courthouses to many different groups. More specifically, justices who want to reach a certain decision on the merits allow that to determine whether or not they will enforce the rules of access. Typically, allowing cases to proceed regardless of justiciability issues means that the Court will be permitting the have-nots of society to have more access to its dockets.

A few examples demonstrate the flexibility of justiciability. Opponents of certain policies have tried to use the courts when their pleas have been ignored by the elected branches. In *Frothingham v. Mellon* (1923), a citizen from Massachusetts challenged a federal act that forced states to comply with certain regulations. Frothingham argued that the law, which did not affect her directly, nonetheless violated due process of the law. She claimed that because she was a taxpayer and her taxes went to support the program, she had standing to challenge the law. Traditionally, the Supreme Court has enforced the requirement that the parties to a case must have standing. In this case, the Supreme Court, adopting judicial restraint, claimed that paying taxes did not provide her with standing. Rather, the Court ruled that the small amount of her taxes that went to the policy she opposed did not entitle her to sue. She had failed to prove that she suffered a direct injury (Epstein and Walker 1998a, 103–104). The Court dismissed the case without considering the merits of her claim.

The activist Warren Court was responsible for loosening the standing requirements in *Flast v. Cohen* (1968), allowing taxpayers to challenge state aid to a parochial school as a violation of the Establishment Clause of the First Amendment. Judicial activism and the willingness to address an important constitutional issue was the motivation for suspending the standing requirements.

Lowering the standing requirements was an invitation for cases challenging government policies. It also meant that the Court would be risking confrontations with the elected branches of government if it allowed taxpayers to challenge policies they did not like. Indeed, the Court was asked by a taxpayer who wanted to obtain details of the activities and expenditures of the Central Intelligence Agency (Fisher 1988, 98–99). In *United States v. Richardson* (1974), the Burger Court held that the plaintiffs lacked standing to challenge the policies. Discretion became the better part of valor when the Court refused to be tempted to climb out on a limb that could not support such judicial interference.

The Burger Court could have dismissed the *Roe v. Wade* case had a majority of the justices desired. The case took more than two years to develop. Jane Roe, the pseudonym for Norma McCorvey, had either had the baby or did not. Her specific claim became moot by the passage of time. A majority, anxious to decide the issue or resigned to having to consider the case, chose to ignore the possible defect and address the merits of the abortion question. The Court could have avoided the issue indefinitely by enforcing mootness. It is unlikely that many cases could wind through the lower courts and be decided by the Supreme Court in less than nine months.

At about the same time, the Court used mootness to avoid consideration of affirmative action. In *DeFunis v. Odegaard* (1974), a white student challenged the affirmative action program that excluded him from the University of Washington Law School. By the time the case reached the Supreme Court, Marco DeFunis was in his third year of law school, so there was nothing that the Court could do for DeFunis. Four justices, aware that it was merely a matter of time before a properly constructed affirmative action case was before them, wanted to ignore the mootness problem and address affirmative action directly. Restraint won out by a single vote (Epstein and Walker 1998a, 90–91).

The ripeness doctrine was a wedge that Southern school districts attempted to utilize to thwart school desegregation. A number of the plans developed by school districts to circumvent the *Brown* decision established procedural mazes that would force the parents of African American students to jump through a number of hoops and meet with a number of officials and administrative boards. Invariably, the parent would miss one of the "necessary" boards or the process would take so long that either the school year would almost be over or the student had moved to the next grade. One of two problems would result: The school boards could argue that the case was not ripe because the parents missed a stage of the process, or the case would be moot because the student moved to another grade. The Court saw the Southern school board plans as an attempt to create barriers that would, in effect, deny the parents any chance to get into court, and so refused to enforce the norm.

The Court is not supposed to consider collusive cases because there are no adversary parties. There are no guarantees, however, that the Court will dismiss such cases. The case *Muskrat v. United States* (1911) resulted from a law involving Native American lands. Congress, uncertain whether the law was constitutional, authorized a number of Native Americans who would be affected, including David Muskrat, to challenge the law. The Court, which saw through this attempt to obtain an advisory opinion on the viability of the law, dismissed the suit because it was a collusive or feigned case.

On the other hand, some important constitutional landmarks came from collusive cases that the Supreme Court was willing to decide. The Court declared the federal income tax unconstitutional in *Pollock v. Farmer's Loan and Trust Co.* (1895), a feigned case in which a stockholder tried to stop the corporation from paying a tax thought to be illegal (Pritchett 1984b, 158). A major early New Deal case, *Carter v. Carter Coal Co.* (1936), was a collusive case in which the plaintiff sued his father's company. Both sides in the case sought the same decision: the invalidation of New Deal legislation. The activist Court accepted the case and gave the collusive parties the remedy they sought (Epstein and Walker 1998a, 90).

Every ten years, the government counts its citizens. The law requires a census to determine population and demographic shifts. During the first part of the twentieth century, the population moved from rural areas and small towns into the cities. Most states, however, did not redraw legislative boundaries as a matter of course. As a result, over time, there were tremendous disparities in the population of legislative and congressional districts. Some large cities would elect one representative, while a town with a fraction of the population would have one representative as well. The power of the cities was diminished by their lack of representation.

With that as a backdrop, some concerned citizens went to the Supreme Court to ask the justices to remedy the inequalities, seeking relief in the form of legislative reapportionment. *Colegrove v. Green* (1946) involved the issue of legislative districts in Illinois that were not redrawn after population shifts. The Supreme Court exercised judicial restraint by refusing to address the question of legislative reapportionment, ruling it was a political question.[4]

Less than two decades later, the Court revisited the issue in *Baker v. Carr* (1962). This time, a majority of the justices did not let the political questions doctrine stop them from addressing the substantive issue in the case. In doing so, the Court ruled that Tennessee must reapportion its legislative districts to conform to population shifts. Earl Warren called the decision the most important of his tenure, which is quite impressive given that his Court decided *Brown*, *Mapp v. Ohio*, and *Miranda v. Arizona*, among other landmarks (Cortner 1970). *Baker v. Carr* would provide greater political power for urban areas and help minorities. The activist decision, though, brought a firestorm of protest against the Court, punctuated by congressional threats to the Court's jurisdiction and attempts to pass a constitutional amendment to overturn the decision.

The decision to hear a case despite its irregularities was normally the result of the Court's desire to confront the substantive issue in that case. Enforcement of the rules of access meant that the issue would not be considered. The Court could do nothing about reapportionment until it removed the hurdle of the political questions doctrine. In another example, in 2000, some of the justices argued that the Court should refuse to hear *Bush v. Gore* because it did not meet the rules of access. There were concerns that the case was not ripe and that it was a political question. In the end, the majority disagreed.

Thus, activism begets activism and restraint begets restraint. If the Court decides to enforce the rules of access in refusing to take a case, it is upholding the work of the elected branches. On the other hand, judicial activism, which means that the Court does not enforce the rules of access, allows the Court to consider and attack the work of the elected branches. Judicial activists are willing to lower the procedural hurdles that limit litigation so that they can address the important issues of the day. Judicial activism argues that judges ought to decide cases to further their conception of justice and not avoid them (Wolfe 1997, 2–3). Proponents of restraint would enforce the rules and limit access to the judiciary.

In general, the Warren Court was willing to ignore the rules of access so it could address the substantive issues of the day and, in doing so, provide a forum for the downtrodden of society. It was metajudicial activism. The Warren Court was willing to ignore substantive precedents as well as the precedents that enforced the rules of access in order to address new issues that would overturn the policies of the elected branches and expand or create new constitutional protections. The Burger and Rehnquist Courts were somewhat less willing to open their doors to sweeping constitutional questions and more likely to raise the barriers to litigation. They also limited access of the have-nots to the judiciary.

Checks and Balances

The limits and potential limits on justiciability and jurisdiction are only part of a broader concern with the institutional constraints on the Court. The Court has some institutional weaknesses that seem to argue for judicial restraint. The willingness to exercise activism creates the risk that the Court will overstep its boundaries and invites retaliation from the elected branches.

The creation of separation of powers and checks and balances was a prescription for political conflict. As Louis Brandeis noted, "the government was created not for efficiency, but to avoid the arbitrary use of power" (O'Brien 1997, 4). The division of authority between the different branches of government is a source of both strength and weakness for the Court. It is a weakness in that the other branches hold some potentially strong weapons over the Court. At the same time, separation of powers means that the elected branches have some weaknesses as well. Those constraints provided opportunities for the Court to step in and enhance its own base of power over time.

Perhaps the greatest limitation on the Supreme Court is that the judiciary cannot enforce its own decisions. It lacks "the sword and the purse." Congress has the purse, the president has the sword. If either or both disagree with the Court's decision, that decision may be undermined or not enforced—and either one can retaliate against the Court in a number of ways.

On the face, the legislative and executive branches hold some impressive checks over the Supreme Court. The president has the power of appointment. As discussed in previous chapters, the interpretation of statutes and constitutional provisions and the way existing precedents are handled contribute to the construction of public policy. As a consequence, presidents can exert enormous power over the direction of the Supreme Court through their appointments. On average, a president gets to appoint a justice once every two years. Thus, a one-term president is expected to appoint two justices; two terms may mean four justices, almost a majority. If a Court is closely divided, one or two judicial appointments can dramatically change the membership and decisional trends.

One of the most telling editorial cartoons published during the 1984 campaign showed nine justices who looked exactly like Ronald Reagan sitting on the Supreme Court bench chanting, "Forty more years." The message was reminiscent of one that Richard Nixon often acknowledged: Presidents come and go, but the Supreme Court endures. If presidents use the appointment power wisely, the impact can outlast their tenure by decades.

The president can use his nomination to send a message to the sitting justices or a message about the Court as an institution. Presidents may send a very ideological nominee to try to pull the center of gravity on the Court in a different direction. Presidents have occasionally used a nominee to embarrass the Court as an institution. For example, although he turned out to be one of the great justices, Senator Hugo Black was nominated by Franklin Roosevelt to enrage the Senate and diminish the Supreme Court (Powe 2000, 5). Some view Nixon's failed nomination of G. Harrold Carswell as a similar attempt to embarrass the Senate and lower the prestige of the Court. While one might consider it a good strategy to diminish one's enemies, weakening the Court carries potential consequences that will outlive the term of the president.

As chief executive, the president heads the branch of government that must implement a Court directive. As the voice of the people and one of only two nationally elected officials, the president can use the bully pulpit to help garner public support for the Court's decisions. On the other hand, the president's silence or active opposition to the Court's pronouncement can undermine that decision.

Few things hurt the Court's legitimacy more than having the president refuse to implement the decision or announce his opposition. There is the example of outright defiance in *Worcester*. In most circumstances, though, presidents support the Court's decisions. In 1974, after the Court ordered Nixon to turn over the Watergate tapes, there was concern that he might destroy them. Instead he complied with the decision, virtually ensuring the end of his tenure. Although few presidents defy the Court, some have been less than effusive in their support of Court decisions. Nixon vowed to implement the Court's desegregation and busing decisions, but as narrowly as possible. Whether they enforce the decision or try to undermine it depends to some degree on whether the decision represents activism or restraint. Presidents are less likely to have concerns with decisions that are restraintist in orientation.

Congress is not a passive participant in the system of checks and balances. It possesses a number of formal and informal checks on the Court. It shares appointment authority with the president in that the Senate must confirm the nomination. The Senate has the power to advise and consent. This check seems to be directed more at the president than the Court, but the authority to confirm or deny an appointment has important implications for the Court as well. The Senate has been more active since the 1980s, rejecting a number of nominees and making the confirmation of others more uncertain. The Senate's rejection of Robert Bork's nomination in 1987 was directed at the president, to be sure, but it was also a function of the balance on the Court. Bork was nominated to replace a moderate, Lewis Powell. Senate Democrats feared that Bork would tip the Court too far in the conservative direction. The willingness of Congress to exert the power may have also had an impact on the types of nominees recent presidents have put forward (Abraham 1999).

In some instances, the Senate's response is not so much a reaction to a particular candidate as it is a referendum on the sitting Court. During the Warren Court, the Senate would make nominees jump through some additional hoops as a means of sending a thinly veiled message to the other eight justices. Activism and restraint play a role. If the Senate detects a streak of activism in the nominee, the road to confirmation will be more problematic.

Congress's purse is another check. While some decisions require congressional resources to implement, the budget has other ramifications as well. The Constitution does not permit Congress to reduce the salaries of sitting justices, but Congress can send a message of displeasure by refusing to give the justices a raise or by giving them a raise that is decidedly less than the increases given to lower federal court judges. Each year, the Court sends a justice or two to Capitol Hill to argue on behalf of its budget. There is one clear rule of thumb: Judicial activists need not apply. The Court usually sends less controversial proponents of judicial restraint, such as Justice O'Connor, to avoid antagonizing the Appropriations Committees.

While budget power is largely symbolic, the power to reverse a statutory judicial decision often is not. When the Court makes a decision that involves interpreting a statute, Congress may well disagree with the interpretation. If there is disagreement, then Congress may overrule the Court's interpretation. To do so, Congress requires only a simple majority in both houses. The Court issued a very narrow interpretation of Title IX, which Congress eventually overturned, as noted in Chapter 1. After the Supreme Court decided that pregnancy was not a protected disability under the Civil Rights Act, Congress passed the Pregnancy Discrimination Act in 1978 to reverse the decision (Hoff 1991, 294–298).

Not all reversals of Court decisions carry a stigma. Sometimes, the Court honestly does not know what Congress intended or how the statute applies to unforeseen circumstances. In such cases, the Court may invite Congress to correct its interpretation of the statutory provisions (Hauseggar and Baum 1999).

The interpretation of statutes by the Court raises one dimension of the dilemma of policymaking. Judicial activism occurs when a Court dramatically expands or contracts statutory provisions and that is bound to raise the ire of Congress. With that in mind, analysts note that the Court pays close attention to Congress and how it might react to a particular interpretation. The Court acts strategically to move its decisions from its desired point to a position closer to congressional desires. In doing so, the Court avoids congressional retaliation that could affect its legitimacy (Eskridge 1994).

It stands to reason that to stick close to the statute represents restraint and does not antagonize the elected branches. But does it? William Eskridge argues that the process works, but with a twist. When the Court interprets statutory provisions, it responds not to the Congress that authored the bill, but to the sitting Congress, the one that could retaliate against a decision it did not like. In its expansive interpretation of the Civil Rights Act of 1964, the moderate-to-conservative Burger Court was responding to the positions of the liberal Congress that was in power rather than the intent of the Congress that created the landmark legislation.

If the Court bases its decision on constitutional grounds, the task for undoing it is daunting. To overturn a constitutional decision, Congress must initiate the process of a constitutional amendment. The problem for Congress is that getting an amendment to the ratification stage requires the votes of two-thirds of both houses of Congress. It has happened: The Eleventh, Thirteenth, Fourteenth, and Twenty-Sixth Amendments were ratified to overcome Supreme Court decisions. However, that is a tiny fraction of all the attempts to initiate constitutional amendments that have failed. Since the 1970s, proposed amendments to ban abortion, busing, and flag burning and to permit school prayer all failed.

Congress has means of dealing with Court decisions short of actually overturning them. As discussed earlier, Congress can tamper with the Court's jurisdiction. In addition, Congress can introduce blocking legislation to limit the impact of a decision it opposes. Not long after *Roe v. Wade*, Congress—unable to muster the extraordinary majorities necessary for a constitutional amendment to overturn the decision—passed the Hyde Amendment, which was an amendment to a bill, not the Constitution. This provision cut off federal funds for abortions. The decision did not overturn *Roe*, but it clearly made the exercise of reproductive rights more difficult (Hoff 1991, 302–305).

Congress has a few extraordinary checks that it can use against the Court. First, as there is nothing magical about the number nine, Congress can alter the size of the Court. When the Civil War began, Congress added three justices to the seven already on the bench for the sole purpose of giving Abraham Lincoln a working majority. After the Civil War, the Radical Republicans in Congress did not want Andrew Johnson to have the opportunity to fill any vacancies, and so reduced the size of the Court from ten to nine to eight and, finally, to seven justices. When Ulysses Grant was elected, Congress raised the number to its current nine (O'Brien 2000, 364).

After a term of frustration marked by Court resistance to his New Deal programs and now with a reelection landslide mandate in his pocket, Franklin Roosevelt proposed his Court Reorganization Plan. The plan would allow for one new justice for every justice over the age of seventy. He said the plan would help a Court that was populated by six elderly justices. In reality, it was a thinly veiled attempt to reconfigure the Court to make it sympathetic to Roosevelt's programs. With the chance to pack the Court with up to six new justices, Roosevelt could almost ensure the success of his programs. The Court-packing plan was a reaction to judicial activism (Pacelle 1991, 49).

The second extraordinary check is impeachment power. Although this is an extreme power that is seldom utilized, there are some historical precedents. Samuel Chase is the only Supreme Court justice to have been impeached. The Jeffersonians targeted this Federalist appointee in 1805. It was widely assumed that if Chase was impeached and convicted, then Chief Justice Marshall would be next. When Chase was acquitted, it established a precedent for a high standard to remove someone from the Court. Part of the attack on Chase was predicated on simple partisan politics, but the subtext was the judicial activism of the Marshall Court in empowering itself and in expanding constitutional provisions (Schwartz 1993, 57–58).

William Douglas, the textbook example of judicial activism, was the subject of the only other serious attempt to impeach a justice. There were two separate impeachment resolutions introduced against Douglas. The first, in 1953, dealt with his willingness to stay the execution of Ethel and Julius Rosenberg, convicted of spying for the Soviet Union. In 1970, Congressman Gerald Ford led the second effort to impeach the maverick justice. Ostensibly, Ford objected to potential conflicts of interest involving Douglas.[5] However, the real reasons behind the proposed impeachment were: a *quid pro quo* for two rejected Republican nominees, and a response to the often outrageous and very liberal Douglas, who had a lifestyle that offended many in the Washington community. Neither of the attacks on Douglas made it out of committee or to the floor of the House (O'Brien 2000, 101–102). Similarly, neither of the impeachment proceedings had any effect in toning down Douglas's private or public life.

Exposing the Supreme Court

In the end, what do all of these checks mean? First, checks do not have to be used to be effective. The political branches hold checks that would seem to be strong arguments for judicial restraint. They also suggest that if the Court gets too far out of step with public opinion, there will presumably be an outcry that will resonate with Congress and the president and trigger one of the checks.

Sometimes the Court can be led into a trap by the president or Congress. When divided government dominates the American political scene, a president facing congressional resistance may try to use the Supreme Court to push his agenda. Asking the Court to change constitutional interpretation to reflect the president's policy goals or to limit statutes passed by Congress invites judicial activism. This could place the Court in the middle of disputes between a president of one party and a Congress dominated by the other.

Critics have charged that Congress has abdicated its authority in many issue areas. Congress has been unwilling or unable to address the core questions involving abortion, for example. By taking on these issues, the Court leaves itself open to potential retaliation. In the end, Congress gets the best of both possible worlds. Members of Congress are able to avoid very contentious issues that are likely to anger large numbers of people and threaten their chances for reelection. Then after the Court acts, its members can rise in righteous indignation, criticizing the institution that stepped into the vacuum they left.

More recently, Congress and state legislatures have been accused of passing what Michael Bamberger (2000) called "reckless legislation." Bamberger accuses lawmakers of passing patently unconstitutional acts to score political points with voters, knowing that the laws have almost no chance of surviving judicial review. Congress passed, with the blessing of President Clinton, the Communications Decency Act of 1995, but in *Reno v. American Civil Liberties Union*, the Supreme Court unanimously found the legislative restrictions on the Internet wanting. By passing such laws, the elected branches invite judicial review and activism. This creates a no-lose situation for members of Congress: They can pass a popular law that is clearly unconstitutional and then critique the Court for striking a law that they can claim their constituents wanted.

Legitimacy is tied to the Court's visibility or lack thereof. Activism begets visibility. The Court has often been responsible for placing the spotlight on itself by actively involving itself in the issues of the day. That activism has threatened the Court on more than a few occasions. The Court shined a very public spotlight on itself in deciding *Bush v. Gore*. Whether the enhanced visibility and the controversy that came with it has long-term effects remains to be seen.

The advent and increase of "reckless legislation" is a different phenomenon, but it could have similar results. A hot-button issue can force the Supreme Court to take the unpopular, but the legally correct, position, which raises the visibility of the Court and exposes it to attack from the elected branches and the public—a clear threat to the Court's legitimacy.

Legitimacy is also a function of the Court's willingness to stretch the boundaries of its power. Obviously, those boundaries can change and the Court's policy-making discretion can expand with the different times and issues. The Court's willingness to protect the rights of insular minorities when no other branch would step forward was justified by the needs of the time. At other times, the Court exercised restraint or risked self-inflicted wounds, such as with *Dred Scott* and the early New Deal.

The Power and Potential
of the Supreme Court

The limitations on the Supreme Court are very real and seem to suggest that the justices should adopt judicial restraint. However, the Court is not completely helpless and not without its own resources. Indeed, the Supreme Court has become a rather powerful institution despite weaknesses that existed from its inception. The Court does not have an impressive set of formal powers, but the major power, judicial review, has given the Court the opportunity to stretch its authority in a variety of directions. While judicial review is a significant power, its force lies more in its potential than in its actual use. It is a power akin to the executive veto. The mere existence of this power often serves as a deterrent to prevent the passage of questionable legislation.

By virtue of judicial review, the Court has accrued other power. On a day-to-day basis, the authority that is derived from its less formal powers is probably more imposing and more important. The Constitution appears to make the Court the arbiter of its provisions. Marshall certainly argued that this power belonged to the Court. The Warren Court extended this in *Cooper v. Aaron* (1958), when it "claimed not only the right to interpret the Constitution but the right to be final, that is, to bind not only the parties, but everyone else." According to Lucas Powe (2000, 160), "The Constitution, the Court asserted, meant exactly what the Court said it meant." Thus, the Court could make important decisions and policy by interpreting the meaning of constitutional provisions. In constitutional cases, the Court has a great deal of discretion. Because of the extraordinary majorities required to overturn a constitutional decision, the chances of its being overturned are almost nonexistent, placing the Court effectively beyond the reach of the elected branches. The justices also have the opportunity to interpret an ever-growing number of statutory provisions. In each of these instances, the Court can change the meaning of statutes and the Constitution, a measure of activism.

Perhaps of political necessity, the Court became a more potent institution. The defeat of the Federalists in the election of 1800 forced the party to burrow into the judiciary. With an institutional basis, the Federalists had an incentive to empower the judiciary (Schwartz 1993, 37–40). In essence, the Court had to create its own power and that process began in earnest after John Marshall took his place as chief justice in 1801. It would prove to be the creation of a new potential for the judicial branch.

Judicial review has engendered controversy because of its extraconstitutional nature. In *Marbury*, Marshall reasoned that the framers created a Supreme Court and gave it the authority to interpret the Constitution, so they must have intended to give it the power to declare acts of Congress and the president unconstitutional. Judicial review is a potentially significant power, but the Supreme Court did not use it again for another half-century after *Marbury*.

Judicial restraint would argue that justices should be reluctant to utilize this power. Proponents of this position would urge the Court to defer to the elected branches whenever possible. In this view, the Court should only strike down laws that are clearly unconstitutional. In determining which laws are constitutionally suspect, the Court should apply neutral principles that reflect enduring values that created the nation and the Constitution. It suggests a static, unchanging interpretation of the Constitution.

Judicial activism, on the other hand, argues for a more aggressive use of judicial review. Activists would not be shy about finding laws unconstitutional. They would be more likely to use judicial review to pursue their goals in the particular cases. Activists would not feel bound by broad, unchanging standards in assessing the constitutionality of laws. Instead, the principles and values used to determine whether a law was constitutional might well change with the times in their view (Wolfe 1997, 30–31). The Constitution, then, becomes a living document.

As Marshall argued, it is implied in the Constitution that the Court shall be the arbiter of the meaning of its provisions. The authority to interpret statutes and the Constitution provides the Court with the opportunity to make public policy.

When the Supreme Court gutted the Fourteenth Amendment at the end of the nineteenth century and then began restoring it in the 1950s, the justices were, in effect, "rewriting" the Constitution. As Justice Jackson remarked, decisions of the Supreme Court are "not final because we are infallible, but we are infallible only because they are final." The Court created the right to privacy and grounded the exclusionary rule, a judge-created remedy, in the Constitution. To change such an interpretation would require a constitutional amendment, a remote possibility.

The Supreme Court also has the power to interpret statutory language. It is a virtual axiom that in order to get a bill passed through Congress, the language has to be vague and open-ended. Responsibility, then, passes to the bureaucracy that has to implement the provisions and to the courts that have to interpret them. When the Supreme Court interprets a statute, the Court, in effect, is thrust into the legislative process. There are rules concerning statutory interpretation, but they are treated as guidelines rather than red-letter commandments. Thus, while there are clear institutional limitations on the power and authority of the Court, by virtue of its position, there is potential for meaningful influence.

The Court has an additional resource to draw upon: the widespread recognition that the Court has the legitimate authority to interpret the Constitution. This provides a great deal of institutional respect for the Court. The president of the United States stands on the steps of the Capitol and takes an oath to uphold the Constitution. Members of Congress swear to uphold the Constitution as well. Underlying that is the notion that the Court's interpretation of the Constitution in a particular case becomes the law of the land. Presidents and members of Congress may well oppose decisions of the Court, but it is a big step to attack the Court or undermine its authority. The Court has some allies, whether they be short-term (groups and officials who support the controversial decision) or long-term (the general reluctance to attack a respected institution).

As a practical matter, over the past half-century, the American system has been dominated by divided government. The electorate continues to send one party to the White House and the other to Capitol Hill. Under these conditions, one party and one branch of government are likely to protect the Supreme Court. This has coincided with a more activist Court. More broadly, the Court has a symbolic aura surrounding it that protects it from the reach of the other branches to some degree. Partially because it is the least understood branch of government, it has the highest level of public support. Because of the legal nature of the Court and the trappings of the institution, the Court earns a high measure of respect from the public. That diffuse support translates to the legitimacy of the Supreme Court as an institution—its ultimate resource and most important base of power. The Court's decisions need to be accepted as "proper." The legitimacy of the Court rests on its ability to remain faithful to the law. The Supreme Court needs to preserve its legitimacy "in the public's eyes and thereby encourages the public to respect and obey judicial decisions" (Smith 1997, 20).

Therein lies the rub, however. The Court needs to protect its legitimacy. The best way to do that is to exercise judicial restraint. In practical terms, this would translate to enforcing the rules of access, being very reluctant to use judicial review, paying faithful attention to statutory language, and upholding precedent. The Supreme Court needs to be seen as a court, not a superlegislature. As Christopher Smith (1997, 6) argues, "If courts do not preserve their distinctiveness from other political bodies, if they cease being 'courts,' then their claim to legitimacy—and their power—will erode."

On the other hand, a wholesale adoption of judicial restraint might be considered to be judicial abdication. The Court needs to strike an appropriate balance between respect for the prerogatives of the elected branches and activism when it is necessary. In some areas, most notably, the protection of individual liberties, the Court might be considered the dominant actor. If that is the case, the Court might reserve its judicial activism for civil rights and civil liberties cases.

There is evidence that the Court does adopt some forms of judicial restraint. The use of judicial review is sparing. Precedents are seldom overturned outright. Some analysts argue that the Court acts strategically when it makes some of its decisions, particularly those that involve statutory interpretation (Eskridge 1994; Epstein and Knight 1998). In those cases, the Court's decision can be overturned by a bare majority of both houses. The notion of strategic decisionmaking is that the Court will react to the position of Congress and make a decision that is closer to that than the position the justices might adopt if they were unconstrained. This would reduce the chances that Congress would overturn the Court's decision. If such strategic decisionmaking does occur, then it would represent some attention to democratic concerns in respecting the prerogatives of the elected branches.

Conclusion

There are two sets of constraints on the Court: internal and external. They appear to place the Court in a potentially vulnerable position. The internal constraints, process and justiciability, invite the justices to exercise self-restraint. Judicial restraint means that the justices would enforce the rules of access and not decide cases with justiciability problems. Justices who want to exercise activism and decide the cases on their docket can ignore the defects in the case and decide the substantive issues. Thus, the question of activism and restraint lies in the hands of the justices. Process questions are the subject of the next chapter.

The other constraints involve threats to the Court's jurisdiction and other checks from external forces. Such checks are seldom used, in part because the Court does not often provoke the other branches to exercise them. Situational activism tempered by general restraint can provide the Court with latitude and allow it to keep the other branches at bay.

The uncertainty over the role of the Court was reflected in *The Federalist* 78. In one section, Alexander Hamilton argued that the Court has many constraints on its power. Lacking the power to implement its decisions puts the judiciary in a vulnerable position. Hamilton wrote, "It may truly be said to have neither the force or the will, but merely judgment; and must ultimately depend upon the aid of the executive arm for the efficacy of its judgment."

On the other hand, in the same essay, Hamilton recognized the potential that the judiciary may achieve: "The interpretation of the laws is the proper and peculiar province of the courts. A constitution is, in fact, and must be regarded by the judges as a fundamental law. It therefore belongs to them to ascertain its meaning, as well as the meaning of any particular act proceeding from the legislative body." Indeed, this becomes the real source of the Court's power: the authority to interpret the Constitution and statutes.

The Court has formal powers that can be brought to bear in potential conflicts with the other branches of government. Most notably, there is the power of judicial review. The potential of the authority is often enough to lead Congress or the president to kill problematic bills. More prevalent is the authority to determine what a statute or a constitutional provision means. The process by which Congress passes laws ensures that statutory provisions will need interpretation. Similarly, the vagueness of the Constitution requires translation into real-world issues and problems. Those practical concerns raise the question of whether the Constitution should be adapted to the times. It is often the Supreme Court that has to decide that question. In interpreting the Constitution, the Court has broader leeway and the prospects for reversal are quite limited. In statutory construction, the Court walks a fine line between restraint and activism.

The limitations on the Court are not as significant as they once seemed. They constrain the Court, but the boundaries of those constraints are very broad. Justiciability is self-imposed and seems to be a function of the composition of the Court, rather than a philosophical position. Checks and balances are seldom successfully invoked against the judiciary, in part because the Court has positive institutional resources to justify its decisions. The Supreme Court has a relatively high level of diffuse support that comes, in part, from a general lack of knowledge by the public and that contributes to its legitimacy.[6] The cloak of the Constitution and the symbolism attendant to the marble palace and the law contribute as well. As a result, presidents and Congress should pause before striking at the Court or refusing to follow its directives. Indeed, presidents and members of Congress can often use unpopular Court decisions as political cover. They cite the need to enforce or support such decisions even though they disagree with them. In the end, the institutional limitations do not mandate judicial restraint, but turn the focus to judicial capacity, the subject of the next chapter.

Notes

1. See Irons 1990 for more on the case.

2. The Air Force Reservists, who organized to oppose military involvement, alleged injury because members of Congress holding positions in the Reserves were subject to undue influence by the executive branch and might not discharge their duties as legislators.

3. Presidents have used the "vesting" and "take care" clauses to expand their power.

4. Part of the reason for refusing to consider the case was that it was so close to the election that some justices did not want to interfere.

5. Douglas's stockholding in a company was part of the reason. Justice Abe Fortas had recently been pushed from the Court in part because of some of his holdings. Douglas was also charged with a failure to recuse or exclude himself from some Supreme Court cases involving obscenity charges against a magazine that published excerpts from his book, *Points of Rebellion* (O'Brien 2000, 101–103).

6. Brigham (1987) maintains that the Court is perceived to follow the adage laid out by Charles Evans Hughes, "We live under a Constitution, but the Constitution is what the judges say it is." At the same time, despite the fact that the Court may act like an outright political institution, the Court is perceived as a legal institution and thus remains insulated and somewhat removed from politics.

5

The Judicial Capacity Dimension of the Dilemma: Does the Supreme Court Have the Ability to Make Policy?

The arguments about judicial capacity are the empirical side of the normative institutional argument. The Supreme Court is said to lack capacity in large part due to the weaknesses of the judiciary. Because the Court lacks the sword and the purse and must rely on the elected branches, it starts with a significant disadvantage as a policymaker. The notion of capacity is an attempt to see if the Court can overcome those disadvantages. If it cannot, then the remedy is judicial restraint. Consider an example from a famous decision.

Brown v. Board of Education (1954) was a true landmark decision. In its opinion, the Supreme Court unanimously held that in the realm of education, separate but equal had no place. The Court tried to help a whole class of citizens overcome long-standing regional policies and prejudices. Many thought that the Supreme Court was not up to the monumental task and that tackling the issue was beyond the capacity of the judiciary.

The Court faced a number of problems. Someone had to monitor the implementation of *Brown*, a task left to the federal district courts. The courts did not have the resources to ensure that school districts complied with the desegregation orders. In addition, the judicial process is protracted, meaning that challenges to the desegregation orders would need to be tried in the district court and then be appealed to the Supreme Court.[1] Thus, it would take a great deal of time to evaluate each challenge to the integration policies. Southern opponents of desegregation were only too happy to take advantage of this process.

The structural problems that the Supreme Court typically faces all but guaranteed that there would be severe implementation problems, particularly given the massive undertaking of school desegregation. Although the Court's decision was a tremendous symbolic statement for civil rights, the practical effects of the decision were limited by Southern opposition. Fifteen years after the decision, very little had been done to desegregate Southern schools. Arguably, nothing happened until Congress passed the Civil Rights Act of 1964 and President Johnson threw the moral authority of his office behind the decision.

Brown and subsequent civil rights decisions did achieve one thing: They raised expectations that equality would emerge. Gerald Rosenberg (1991, chapters 3–4) argued that the Supreme Court actually did more harm to civil rights by announcing the *Brown* decision. He claimed that if the Court had not intervened in

1954, Congress and the president would have been forced to step into the vacuum sooner and more forcefully. Instead the Court thrust itself into a controversial issue without the wherewithal to achieve its lofty goals. The argument has been advanced that this task was beyond the capabilities of the judiciary, given its institutional weaknesses. The capacity of the Supreme Court to make coherent public policy is assessed in this chapter.

The Supreme Court: Powerful Enough or Too Weak?

Earl Warren presided over a constitutional revolution. Besides the *Brown* decision, the Supreme Court that bore his name reapportioned state legislatures, changed police procedures, and created a constitutional right to privacy. The Burger Court extended equal protection to gender issues, created reproductive rights, erected a high but serpentine wall between church and state, and created a variety of remedies such as busing to achieve racial integration and affirmative action (Maltz 2000).

These decisions were clear examples of judicial activism. They also presented a picture of the Supreme Court as perhaps the most potent policymaker in the governmental system. Even if the Court was not the most effective, it seemed to be the branch most willing to tackle the controversial issues of the time. At first blush, the Court's decisions suggest a powerful institution that succeeded, to some degree, in integrating Southern schools, providing some measure of equality for women, and protecting defendants' rights.

These examples reflect what Rosenberg (1991, 22) refers to as the Dynamic Court View. Groups and individuals have turned to the courts when the other branches turned a deaf ear. The unelected nature of the Court frees it from the electoral and institutional constraints that pose barriers to change. The elected branches may be unwilling or unable to proceed, and there are electoral consequences for addressing controversial issues or aiding unpopular minorities. Southern senators, for instance, could block any consideration of civil rights. Legislators would never support reapportionment when it could cost them their jobs.

The Dynamic Court View holds that the judiciary can serve as a catalyst for policy change. The Court can address issues that the other branches ignore and place them on the public agenda. The Court's decisions can mobilize groups to exercise their rights and may even spur action from the other branches of government. The Court can force issues onto the agenda of busy representatives and raise issues that politics-as-normal might block from consideration. Defenders of this role believe that litigation and the courts serve as catalysts, not usurpers of the legislative process (McCann 1994; Epp 1998).

The countervailing perspective is referred to as the Constrained Court View. As a consequence of the institutional problems identified in Chapter 3, many subscribe to this view. Rosenberg (1991, 10–21) argues that the Constrained Court View is premised on three factors. The first constraint is that the limited nature of constitutional rights prevents the Court from hearing or acting effectively on broad social issues and diminishes the chances of support from the other branches and the public. There are limits to the types of claims that can be based on rights. To pursue policies, the Court may have to "create" new rights, which is a problematic task. In addition, framing issues to meet the requirements of the judiciary may limit their political appeal. It may drain the issue of the emotional appeal necessary to attract political and public support.

The second constraint is based on the notion that the Court lacks the necessary independence from the executive and legislative branches to make effective public policy. The appointment process limits the independence of the judiciary. Changing the justices can bring the Court into line with the dominant political philosophies. Historically, the Court does not stray far from what is politically acceptable at the time. As the aphorism goes, the Supreme Court follows the election returns. In general, the Court cannot stand for long against the will of the elected branches.

The final constraint holds that the Court lacks the ability and resources to develop policies that will ensure implementation of its decisions. The organizational hierarchy of the courts is not a particularly powerful vehicle for ensuring compliance or implementation. While no judge wants to be reversed on appeal, the chances the Supreme Court will review a lower court judgment are remote. The Supreme Court is not well-suited to evaluate policy over time. The justices are bound to case-by-case determinations, making implementation a difficult process.

Which of these perspectives, the Dynamic Court View or the Constrained Court View, is closer to reality? Is the Court able to make coherent public policy and help to engineer social change? Or are the limitations on the Court so great that it is unable to make public policy and may, in fact, cause harm to the groups that use the judicial branch?

The Supreme Court's Ability to Make Policy

Those who believe that the Supreme Court lacks the capacity to make effective public policy contend that the Court should avoid difficult issues that overextend its capabilities. By taking on such issues, the Court risks making promises that it cannot fulfill and risks losing its finite legitimacy. Advocates of judicial restraint would urge the Court to avoid putting itself in potential peril. They cite evidence that demonstrates the failure of the courts to effect positive meaningful policy and see it implemented (see Horowitz 1977).

Judges make public policy. If this book has any unqualified message, it is that one. Of course, there is a full range of policy from broad-level, sweeping policy to small increments that just fill in some gaps. Recognizing that policymaking is inevitable whenever the Supreme Court issues a decision, proponents of judicial restraint would advocate making it in small increments.

The notion that democratic theory and institutional limitations demand judicial restraint is normative in scope. It is a prescriptive argument for how the Court should operate. Arguments can be mustered in favor of restraint and activism, but there is no conclusive proof to support one argument or the other. With concerns over judicial capacity, the debate over the appropriate role of the Court has shifted to the empirical level. An argument is considered empirical if evidence can be marshaled to support or oppose a position. If the evidence demonstrates that the judiciary cannot effectively make public policy, then that is a further indication that the Court should exhibit restraint.

Even those who oppose judicial policymaking are willing to concede that the Supreme Court can be an effective policymaker when it is dealing with a relatively narrow issue confined to two clearly defined litigants and without broad application to a number of unforeseen circumstances. The problem is that the Court gets very few of those cases. Prior to 1925, the Court had to hear every case properly brought to it, whether the case was important or less profound. Once the Court got discretion, however, the justices began denying petitions to hear minor cases that did not have broad societal impact. Rather, their attention has increasingly been directed to the major issues of the moment. The decisions involve the two parties to the case, but have implications for many similarly situated groups and individuals. As the stakes get higher, the risk for the Court is greater.

How is judicial capacity defined? According to Cavanagh and Sarat (1980, 375), "Court capacity refers to the fit between what courts are and what they do: to the way in which the resources, expertise, and procedures of the courts bear on their ability to provide effective resolution of the cases they handle." As the judiciary deals with increasingly difficult issues, the gap between what the courts are and what they can achieve grows.

One of the critiques of the Court is that it is all too willing to thrust itself into the center of polycentric, redistributive issues. Redistributive issues are the most controversial in American politics. They seek to take some value from one part of society and redistribute it to another. The race cases in the South sought to break the white establishment's hold on political power and redistribute a share of it to African Americans.

A polycentric, or many-centered, issue refers to a multifaceted issue that has many dimensions to it. Donald Horowitz (1977, 59–60) claims that these issues are like webs, and when a judicial decision seems to pull at one part of the web, it has ripple effects that may go in a variety of unintended directions. Those who feel that the courts lack capacity say judges should avoid polycentric issues, but if they cannot, they should decide those cases narrowly and avoid sweeping pronouncements that may solve one problem and create a half-dozen more.

The capacity arguments, which are relatively recent additions to the debate concerning judicial policymaking, arose during the Warren and Burger Courts, when the justices demonstrated a willingness to tackle the most controversial issues and expand constitutional rights. The Warren Court changed judicial decisionmaking in some significant ways. The Court was more willing than its predecessors to permit the introduction of social science factors into legal arguments. The Warren Court changed the nature of civil rights, created federal authority for equal protection, reinvented habeas corpus, invented the constitutional right of privacy, and extended incorporation of the Bill of Rights (Powe 2000). The Burger Court extended the net of equal protection beyond race and supported the broad use of remedies, such as busing and affirmative action (Maltz 2000, 177–185).

The Warren and Burger Courts were often praised for their attempts to achieve justice and extend liberties and rights for many of the downtrodden. The decisions represented important symbols of inclusion and expanded participation in American politics and government. These decisions were not free of controversy, though. The Warren and Burger Courts were criticized for "inventing" constitutional protections and expanding existing provisions well beyond the framers' intent—the "modern" form of judicial activism. Other critiques focused on the extent of the Court's policymaking. The justices were often trying to tailor constitutional remedies to entire classes of people (McDowell 1982). Some of the criticism was directed at the results of the Court's handiwork. The justices raised expectations with their civil rights decisions, but the sad truth was that the cause of equality did not advance as far as the Court seemed to promise. This last critique gets to the heart of the capacity issue.

Assessing Judicial Capacity

One means of evaluating the capacity of the courts to make public policy is to look at the interpretation, implementation, and impact of judicial decisions. If the Court's decisions do not remedy the problems being litigated, then that is a sign that the Court lacks capacity to render successful decisions. Interpretation refers to the process by which lower court judges apply Supreme Court precedents to similar fact situations. In the short-to-medium term, one can address whether the decision was faithfully implemented by the administrators and bureaucrats charged with carrying out the Court's dictates. In the longer term, there is the question of whether the Court's decisions had the desired impact or met the goals of the decision (Canon 1991, 437–441). Figure 5.1 shows the relationship between interpretation, implementation, and impact and suggests that compliance concerns get more difficult as they get further from the Supreme Court's decision.

Judicial decisions are not self-fulfilling directives. Because of institutional limitations, courts cannot implement their own decisions. Thus, the Court must rely on other individuals and institutions to carry out its directives. Because of these potential problems, many argue that the Court should not be active in policymaking. Ultimately, it is an empirical question, like broader notions of capacity. If the justices make decisions that lower courts do not apply or implementers ignore, there is a loss of institutional legitimacy for the Court.

Often there are problems in that a lower court mistakenly applies the wrong precedent or deliberately shirks its responsibilities and misrepresents the Supreme Court's decisions. Implementers may fail to carry out the decision faithfully or undermine it. Finally, the Court's decisions may have little or no impact or may have unanticipated consequences that fail to achieve or, in some cases, contradict the Court's intended goals. The problems with interpretation, implementation, and impact grow as the issues the Court confronts become more complex and controversial. If lower court judges, implementers, and the other branches agree with the Supreme Court's decisions or are indifferent to them, they will support and carry out the decision. If they care about the decision and oppose it, the potential for ignoring the decision grows (Johnson and Canon 1999).

The process of interpreting or implementing a Supreme Court precedent will inevitably reshape the original decision. The lower court may expand or contract the decision. The implementers may carry it out faithfully or ignore the Court. Because standards from one Supreme Court decision must be applied in a number of different jurisdictions and to a number of different factual situations, it is inevitable that the application by lower court judges and implementers with different priorities and goals will not be uniform. That it is not uniform serves to undermine some of the consistency that we seek from law. More troubling perhaps, it means that the Supreme Court cannot assume that its original decision will have the intended effects (Smith 1997, 302). One of the problems for the Supreme Court is that it is difficult for the justices to monitor interpretation, implementation, and impact.

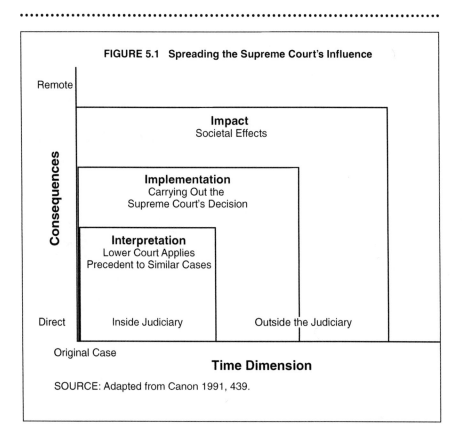

FIGURE 5.1   Spreading the Supreme Court's Influence

Remote

Consequences

Impact
Societal Effects

Implementation
Carrying Out the
Supreme Court's Decision

Interpretation
Lower Court Applies
Precedent to Similar Cases

Direct   Inside Judiciary   Outside the Judiciary

Original Case
Time Dimension

SOURCE: Adapted from Canon 1991, 439.

Of the three sets of concerns, interpretation, implementation, and impact, the problems of faithful compliance grow as one moves further away from the decision. Although interpretation, the manner in which lower courts apply the Supreme Court's precedents, is far from perfect, there are factors that may help the Supreme Court achieve its goals. Most important, lower court judges are socialized to follow the dictates of the Supreme Court. In addition, the Supreme Court has the power of reversal at its disposal, and lower court judges do not want their decisions reviewed or overturned. Compliance does not occur in every circumstance, to be sure, but often lower courts make a good faith effort to comply with the Supreme Court's decisions. In the wake of *Brown*, many Southern judges who were charged with the responsibility of carrying out the decision made substantial efforts to be faithful to the Supreme Court, despite the fact that they disagreed with the decision or were threatened if they tried to follow the precedent (Peltason 1961).

Implementation is quite another story. It is more distant than interpretation in two ways and thus becomes more difficult to monitor. First, it occurs temporally after the lower courts have had their chance to comply. Second, the process of actually carrying out the decision normally requires that the issue leaves the judicial hierarchy. Implementation requires the work of a police officer if it is a criminal justice decision, a doctor or hospital if it is an abortion or health decision, or a teacher if the decision concerns student rights. These implementers have no legal training in interpreting judicial decisions and do not have the socialization experiences that might lead lower court judges to follow a decision they did not support.

An additional problem comes from the values and goals of the individuals who have to implement the decisions. Judges and implementers will normally support and implement decisions that they agree with or that fall into their zones of indifference. The problem is that for most implementers there is no zone of indifference (Johnson and Canon 1999, 162). A Court decision that tells agencies they have to modify their standard operating procedures is likely to be met with resistance. What does the Supreme Court know about the procedures out in the field far removed from Washington D.C.? When the Court tells the police that they have to modify their procedures for interrogation or warrants, the officers are very likely to care about the new requirements. Similarly, teachers will care if the Court tells them that they cannot hold a voluntary moment of silence or prayer. In some instances, those who have to carry out the Court's directive may not know what is required of them. More likely, their lack of a law degree may mean that they know only the basics of the Court's opinion and do not understand all of the legal niceties of the decision.

Because of the temporal and spatial distance, the monitoring problems of the implementation stage are very difficult. The Supreme Court cannot accurately oversee the lower courts, let alone peek into police stations, hospitals, and school classrooms. To review the implementation activities of one of these agents would require a litigant or an organized group to bring a subsequent petition to the Supreme Court's attention.

There are many examples of implementation problems following Supreme Court decisions. The police in many jurisdictions did not implement the warrant requirements of *Mapp v. Ohio* as faithfully as they might. Southern school boards enacted a number of measures to thwart the integration of schools. They closed the public schools, developed freedom of choice plans, established networks of private schools, passed out tuition grants, and generally made implementation almost impossible for more than a decade. In many schools in the Midwest, teacher-led prayer continued unabated despite the Supreme Court's decision in *Engel v. Vitale*. Part of the problem was that in homogeneous school districts, parents supported school prayer and did not try to bring a case to terminate the practice (Johnson and Canon 1999, 75). There are even problems from those who should know better. In *Immigration and Naturalization Service v. Chadha* (1983), the Supreme Court declared the legislative veto unconstitutional, affecting more than a hundred congressional acts that had such veto provisions. In the wake of the decision, Congress continues to use the device and to pass new legislative veto provisions (Devins 1996, 151).

Finally, in the long term, the question can be asked, Has the decision had the consequences that the Court intended? This is removed even further from the Court's decision and may require years before an assessment can be offered. The more difficult the issue, the less likely the Supreme Court's decisions will have the desired impacts. When the Court tackles seemingly intractable social problems that the other branches have failed to address or failed to solve, the prospects of success are remote from the start. The Court's decisions are unlikely to solve these difficult problems, and the Court is branded incapable of making public policy.

The Supreme Court's decisions in desegregating the schools and trying to spread civil rights to housing, employment, and affirmative action were designed to achieve a measure of equality for African Americans. A half-century after *Brown*, few would argue that the Court achieved this goal. Some would suggest that the Court achieved nothing in this area and that only after Congress passed the Civil Rights Act of 1964 and the Voting Rights Act of 1965 was there any movement in civil rights policy (Rosenberg 1991, 41–52). Decisions designed to create gender equality have also fallen short of their goals. Questions have arisen as to the long-term impact of decisions such as *Mapp* and *Miranda*. Have those decisions and others like it handcuffed the police and helped criminals go free? Did they contribute to the steady rise in crime rates in the decade after the Court's decisions?

The problems that the Court faces in interpretation, implementation, and impact threaten the institution's legitimacy and undermine its ability to construct public policy. These shortcomings would make an argument for judicial restraint. On the other hand, these problems are not exclusive to the judicial branch. The public policy literature revealed that implementation and impact problems are endemic to policymaking at all levels, no matter where the policy was constructed. Studies of the congressional and presidential policy initiatives of the Great Society show wholesale failures in implementing the programs and all sorts of unintended consequences (Heath 1975, 280–302).

Part of the problem with the Great Society programs of the 1960s is that they were broad policy initiatives that sought to achieve very ambitious goals. The War on Poverty and other measures tried to alter the fabric of American society. It is little surprise that they failed to achieve their laudable goals or to wipe out poverty (Graham 1990, 266–277). The failure of these policies had two effects.

First, it disappointed the groups that the policies were meant to help, after having raised their expectations. Second, it created a rising belief that government was too big and could not solve certain problems. The broader the goals, the more likely the disappointment. This is a lesson that the judiciary has learned, but it is certainly not confined to the third branch of government (Rosenberg 1991, 359–360).

The Indictment Against the Judiciary

The failures of judicial policymaking are a symptom of a broader set of concerns. Some analysts claim that courts lack the capacity to make public policy effectively. The Constrained Court View holds that the Court has trouble making policy without the assistance of the other branches. The argument against the capacity of the courts centers on the personnel and the judicial process. First, analysts claim that judicial training does not prepare judges for making policy. They contend that judicial procedures do not permit judges to monitor cases, sequence the construction of policy, or evaluate the work that has been done. In other words, justices cannot supervise interpretation and implementation and cannot assess impact. As a consequence, the adversary system is considered a barrier to the coherent building of public policy. Those who believe that the courts lack the capacity to make coherent public policy feel that judges should adopt judicial restraint and cede policymaking to the elected branches and administrators, who presumably have the capacity to construct policy in a more systematic fashion.

According to Donald Horowitz (1977, 18), perhaps the most notable proponent of the view that courts lack the capacity to fulfill their responsibilities, capacity and legitimacy are closely intertwined: "A court wholly without capacity may forfeit its claim to legitimacy." But is the Court "wholly without capacity"? The arguments for and against the thesis that courts lack capacity are listed in Table 5.1.

Personnel: Generalist Judges

The first problem, according to Horowitz (1977, 25–27), is that judges are generalists who are often required to make specialized decisions that will have social consequences. Often judges are required to fill specific gaps in the law, but lack the specialized knowledge to do so. Rather, they are forced to rely on broad normative ideals. The training and socialization of judges does not provide them with expertise on many of the substantive issue areas they face. The lack of expertise means

• •

TABLE 5.1 The Controversy over the Capacity of the Judiciary	
The Case for Judicial Restraint Absolute Capacity	**The Case for Judicial Activism Relative Capacity**
Personnel: untrained generalists	Personnel: advantages of generalists
Adjudication process: undermines coherence	Practical politics limits policymaking
Legitimacy of the other branches	Advantages of the judicial branch
Source: Richard Pacelle.	

that justices are unable to interpret the information they receive (Youngblood and Folse, 1981, 28–31).

Most judges were trained in law school decades before they ascended the bench, and their generalized training was strictly in the law and legal reasoning. They gained the authority to decide policy issues by virtue of their appointment to the bench. Their range of experience before ascending the high bench is more limited and most likely did not include the types of issues that they will need to decide. This problem is exacerbated by the fact that Supreme Court justices increasingly face the full spectrum of difficult issues in American politics. Horowitz (1977) adds that judges are insulated from the sociopolitical context, yet they must make decisions that affect that environment. Judicial ethics prohibit judges from actively engaging the parties in the case or discovering additional factors on their own.

So, in deciding cases concerning abortion rights, justices with no medical background have to determine when a fetus is viable to determine when society can intervene and limit reproductive rights choices. Justices with no experience as police officers try to dictate procedures to those who face the day-to-day dangers of the streets. In economic policy, they may not understand the specific impact of regulatory schemes they have to evaluate in complex areas of law. In short, justices are uninformed about many of the issues that they face.

Procedures: Hindering Policymaking

If judges are relatively uninformed, then the manner in which they get their information in specific cases, the adjudication process, becomes an important concern. Judges must rely on litigants and their expert witnesses for the information they need to make decisions. Each side in a case presents the information most favorable to its cause. If the sides approach the case with unequal resources, then the information presented to the justices may be skewed.

There are questions of legal economy: Courts are not efficient and cost-effective for settling individual disputes. Adjudication is narrow and focused on the individual case, yet a decision from the Supreme Court creates a precedent that will be applied to a number of different cases. The decisions also will be applied by lower courts to a series of different factual situations. Such concerns are exacerbated when courts are asked to reorganize social priorities or deal with broadly based social problems (Wallace 1997, 168). Yet the latter is precisely what the Supreme Court has been asked to do over the last half-century.

The Court's decisions do construct doctrine and public policy over time, but they do so one case at a time. The judicial process is incremental in scope. It is a slow, disjointed process that often appears to move two steps forward and then one step back. The Court is a passive institution, with a very limited ability to sequence innovation or structure the development of cases. As Horowitz (1977, 44) notes, "Because courts respond only to the cases that come their way, they make general law from what may be very special situations." As a consequence, the construction of coherent public policy, built systematically in carefully chosen stages, is very difficult for the courts, constrained as they are by the process and their own institutional limits.

The Supreme Court's decisions often involve the most important social and political issues of the day. However, the judicial process is said to be ill-adapted to gathering social facts. As the Court becomes more activist, its decisions are going to have enormous consequences. This raises concern over the judges' difficulty in getting accurate facts upon which to base decisions that will have a broad impact. There is a great tension for judges between deciding the specific case before them and formulating general policy that will be applicable to unforeseen future factual situations (Horowitz 1977, 47).

In addition, the judicial process makes no provisions for policy review. There is no reliable procedure for ascertaining feedback or determining the unanticipated consequences of decisions. There is no built-in mechanism for correcting problems. Because the courts are not self-starters, they have to rely on litigants to bring subsequent rounds of litigation. If there are interpretation or implementation problems, the Supreme Court will not know unless subsequent cases draw attention to them. The process by which litigants follow up on past decisions is erratic, slow, and uncertain.

Horowitz (1977, 33–37) claims that the judicial process limits the alternatives that judges can consider. The Court can only hear the two parties to the case, each of whom will suggest a potential solution to the legal question before the justices.

The Court's decision will have implications beyond the case even though the facts may not be applicable. On the other hand, before members of Congress and bureaucrats formulate solutions to issues, they are free to consider an entire range of policy alternatives and listen to a number of different voices.

Preferring to avoid general rules that transcend the particular case, the Court follows a "gradual approach to the general by a systematically guarded application and extension of constitutional principles to particular cases as they arise, rather than by out of hand attempts to establish general rules to which future cases must be fitted" (Fisher 1988, 10). At the same time, however, the case creates a precedent that will be applied to other circumstances. Because the Supreme Court can only hear so many cases, it may not have the opportunity to fill in the gaps between precedents.

Viable Alternatives to the Judiciary

The argument that the courts lack capacity means that there are other political actors better suited to make the difficult policy decisions. The bureaucratic agencies are populated by experts and specialists who are trained in the substantive issue areas in which they operate. The congressional committees that make policy recommendations to the entire House and Senate are composed of specialists who have spent years on that committee learning the nuances of the issues they face. Members of Congress have access to an extensive trained staff to help them with their policymaking responsibilities. (Davidson and Oleszek 1997). This is a sharp contrast with most federal judges.

If bureaucrats and members of Congress are better equipped than judges to make decisions, they are also aided by the procedures that govern their behavior. Members of Congress and experts in the agencies have broad access to information that judges lack. Congress holds hearings that allow a wide range of interested parties and relevant agencies to participate and present their views. Once a piece of legislation is passed, the agency has to develop rules and promulgate regulations to enforce it. During that period, there is provision for public comment, allowing the agency to get a range of views to assist them. The agencies and Congress have access to the feedback mechanisms necessary to keep the system moving (Kingdon 1995, 27–34). If there are problems with the law or the execution of it, groups will approach Congress or the bureaucratic agency to have corrections made.

Whereas the Court deals with issues on a case-by-case basis, agencies and Congress are intimately involved with the issue area over time. The Court has to wait for the next case. Agencies and congressional committees can monitor the development of an issue and intervene when they consider it appropriate. They also have the potential for long-term planning. These advantages provide the legislative and executive branches with a potential to make policy in a comprehensive and coherent fashion that the courts cannot hope to match.

As a result, not only are there good normative reasons to allow policy experts and elected officials to make the important substantive policy decisions, there are substantial practical reasons as well. Unlike judges, legislators and bureaucrats are not insulated from the policy environment and have mechanisms for assessing public opinion and social concerns. The other side of the coin is that these factors support arguments for judicial restraint.

The Case for Relative Capacity

While few would accept the Dynamic Court View in its totality, there are analysts who disagree with Horowitz and claim that the courts have the ability to construct public policy in a relatively coherent fashion or, at worst, that the problems courts face are no more daunting than those that affect the other branches. In absolute terms, Horowitz may be correct: The judiciary has some significant problems that suggest a lack of capacity. In relative terms, though, the courts do not appear to fare quite as poorly. I will reassess Horowitz's indictment point by point.

Personnel: The Advantages of Generalists

One of the main criticisms of the courts is the generalist nature of the personnel. Legislators and bureaucrats presumably have more expertise and specialization than judges. However, that is a double-edged sword. Experts and specialists often fall into predictable patterns and develop standard operating procedures that do not permit them to see the larger picture or develop innovative solutions to problems. Policymaking in the United States is often categorized as incremental. A policy response is initially created and passes Congress. Anything that follows in subsequent years is closely related to the initial policy. Alternatives that deviate from that are normally dismissed without serious consideration.

The committee structure in Congress rewards specialization, but at some cost. House committees serve to create legislators who are experts in the areas of their committee assignments but generalists in every other area. This system rewards specialization by asking other members to defer to the experts. Studies of decisionmaking in Congress show that members of Congress take their cues from the specialists (Kingdon 1989).

Expertise and specialization often carry a stigma: The perpetuation of closed policy subsystems has been a bane of the American political structure. In Chapter 3, I discussed the existence and proliferation of subgovernments, the so-called unholy alliances between executive agencies, congressional committees, and interest groups. Specialization provides a stationary target for external interest groups that seek to advance their policy goals. Chairs of committees have risen to their position as a function of seniority, and the heads of the bureaus that are responsible for policy implementation and rulemaking have been in their agencies for a long period of time. As a result, the two groups have interacted over time and know each other intimately. Both know the relevant interest groups that are most concerned about the issue area. All together, they have created the "iron triangles," which political scientists have long argued actually controlled the construction of policy in many issue areas (Riley 1987, 42–44). The argument that legislators and bureaucrats have broader access to information is mitigated to a degree by the fact that they tend to listen only to a select, unrepresentative point of view that supports the status quo.

From the ground up, committees and agencies, with the help of their allies in the private sector, the interest groups, construct public policy far from public view. The final product is supported by the rank-and-file members of Congress who are not experts in the field, but defer to the experts. That procedure of mutual accommodation among members is often referred to as logrolling. The eventual policy comes from a closed system and represents a product that is supported by the closely knit members of Congress, the executive branch, and the interest groups.

Process: Theory Versus Practice

The claim that adjudication is a piecemeal, incremental process is certainly true. By comparison, though, it is hard to argue that the legislative process is very different, if one looks at the results. Legislators often examine policy on a case-by-case basis. Legislation is seldom formulated and adopted in any sort of a comprehensive fashion. It is considered almost an axiom that policymaking in the elected branches is incremental. Budgets and policy initiatives are typically adapted from the previous year with only minor modifications. Even so-called new policies can normally be traced to previous related legislation (Baumgartner and Jones 1993; Kingdon 1995). For both the legislature and the judiciary, most new initiatives are externally derived, the reaction to some crisis or societal developments. In the end, legislative and judicial policymaking are often initiated and shaped by similar circumstances (Smith 1997, 12–13).

The passivity of the Supreme Court is an overrated limitation. Thousands of cases are on the annual docket, and virtually every issue the justices might want to consider is available. The justices have the ability to signal litigants to bring certain types of cases. There are a number of so-called repeat players, long-term actors in the judicial process, who bring cases, respond to the directives and cues in the Court's decisions, and bring the next round of litigation (Galanter 1974). In addition, justices have been known to manipulate the issues in a case to make them more amenable to the type of issues they seek to address. Justices can "add" issues to a case or change the ones that are brought to them (Pacelle 1991, 32–33).

By contrast, Congress has many items on its agenda that are virtually mandatory. Annual budgets have to be passed to keep the government functioning. Legislators are very responsive to interest groups as well, so their passivity represents a difference of degree rather than kind. Bureaucrats formulate regulations after hearings that are dominated by the affected interest groups. The notion of public comment hardly describes reality: "Public hearings" seldom, if ever, involve any of the real public and can be, instead, dominated by interest groups, contributing further to the closed system. Laws are frequently passed in vague language. This requires someone to fill in the details and interpret the provisions, a job that typically falls to the bureaucrats who are unelected (Ripley and Franklin 1982; 1990).

The premise that the courts cannot avoid issues is not completely true at the Supreme Court level. Justices can avoid cases they do not want simply by denying the writ of certiorari. The Court has almost complete discretion over the cases it wishes to take and accepts only a small percentage of the cases properly brought to it. All judges have at their disposal the rules of access—standing, ripeness, mootness, and political questions—as means of avoiding some cases (see Chapter 4). More important, perhaps, judges can narrow the issue in cases, refusing to confront the complex questions directly or withholding their judgment until the issue has percolated in the lower courts for a while longer. Avoiding issues can be a positive attribute. Restraintists often urge the Court to do so. Congress can avoid issues, and many argue that the institution has been loathe to tackle important social issues.

Courts are not completely helpless in getting access to social facts either. The widespread use of *amici* briefs means that the Court will get a range of views on every important issue on its docket. The *amicus curiae,* or "friend of the court," brief permits a group that is not a party to the case to get its views before the Court. The *amicus* brief allows the Court to get a better handle on social facts and assess the broader implications of the case. The *amicus* provides outside expertise for the justices. In *Roe v. Wade,* there were fifty-five *amici* briefs filed by a variety of groups, including those from the medical community, which provided expertise on abortion procedures and the viability of a fetus. In such briefs, groups can expand or narrow the issue in the case beyond the facts and the two parties. In *Regents of the University of California v. Bakke* (1978), involving affirmative action, dozens of colleges and universities provided *amici* briefs to give the Supreme Court some perspective on how the decision would affect them and its potential consequences. More broadly, the briefs provide the Court with an informal tally of public opinion (Pacelle 1991, 31).

With its committees, staffs, and deliberative processes, the legislature would seem better equipped to make judgments about social policies than the courts (Wallace 1997, 167). However, a convincing case can be made for the failure of legislatures to ascertain social facts as well. Specialists and experts are often accused of ignoring information that runs counter to their goals or might threaten standard operating procedures. Committees are often tied to certain groups and administrative agencies over time. Many analysts fault Congress and state legislatures for their parochialism, their abiding concern with reelection and distributive policies, and their utter failure to plan or construct rational policy (Lowi 1979). Once again, the differences between courts and legislatures are more of degree than kind.

The Supreme Court is supposed to have no institutional mechanisms for policy review. The Court is not a self-starter, as noted. It must wait for cases. Legal ethics prohibit judges from the type of *ex parte* communications that are required to assess feedback systematically. The number of interest groups that monitor decisions and stand ready to bring the next case is sufficient to ensure that the Court will have the opportunity to hear most of the cases it needs to follow up previous decisions. The justices can manipulate an existing case by ignoring certain issues or expanding others to help fill the holes in existing doctrine. The Court can also take some extraordinary steps such as hiring a special master to monitor a situation and provide immediate feedback. Courts have done this with prisons and schools to make certain that officials comply with judicial orders.

The Supreme Court can also seek the assistance of the Office of the Solicitor General (and its resources in the Department of Justice) to continue the process of doctrinal development. The solicitor general is the individual who argues the cases for the U.S. government before the Supreme Court. While the solicitor general is a presidential appointee who often does the bidding of the administration, he is a legal actor who must work within the framework provided by the Supreme Court. Indeed, in a number of cases each year, the Court invites the solicitor general's office to provide it with assistance, and in such cases, the solicitor general is expected to provide nonpartisan advice to help the justices with their decision. In any event, the Court does have access to a range of information.

On the face of it, there seem to be significant differences between the abilities of the legislature and the judiciary to get access to feedback and act upon it.

Legislatures can be self-starters, although policy initiatives increasingly come from the executive branch. Legislators can actively seek out information to assess the impact of their handiwork and to make the necessary corrections. In practical terms, though, the differences are not as extensive. One of the roles of Congress is to exercise vigorous proactive oversight of the executive branch—a role that members of Congress have very little incentive to perform. There are few, if any, electoral incentives for members to spend a lot of time on this activity (McCubbins and Schwartz 1984). As with the courts, most of the feedback comes as the result of external actors: litigants, interest groups, or bureaucrats who call the issue to the attention of governmental actors.

Some analysts, like Abram Chayes (1976), maintain that the judiciary has a number of advantages in making public policy. Judges are arguably more neutral and less affected by partisan influences than their legislative counterparts. Courts can be a favorable forum because judges and justices are more insulated from interest groups. Judges can be more flexible in responding to the particular factors present in a given case. Remedies can be constructed to address specific problems in particular cases. Legislation, on the other hand, cannot be tailored in the same way. Statutes tend to paint in broad strokes and require the work of bureaucrats to make them fit particular circumstances.

Chayes argues that the adversary system is more likely to increase the degree of participation. Both sides in a case are guaranteed to have representation. In addition, the use of *amici* briefs, which are found in virtually every important case, expands the level of participation. Both parties have the incentive to get all the relevant facts supporting their sides before the courts and to include like-minded groups. Chayes (1976) claims this is different from the legislative process, which he considers a more closed system. The poor and the have-nots are typically excluded from access to the system. In many areas, well-heeled interest groups have been able to "capture" a particular committee or issue area, and the policy in that area will have their imprint. Conflicting ideas in such closed subsystems are often absent, ignored, or given short shrift.

Finally, judges must respond to the issues that are properly placed on their docket. Through the trial courts and courts of appeal, judges have mandatory jurisdiction and tackle the controversial and complex issues that divide society. They do not have the prerogative that administrators and legislators have in avoiding some issues. For decades, Congress has been accused of avoiding difficult redistributive issues and concentrating on issues that spread benefits to their constituents and help them get reelected. Chayes (1976) believes the judiciary is a less bureaucratic decisionmaking process. Judges hear the complete arguments and are the real decisionmakers. In the legislative and executive branches, policy formulation and legitimation are filtered through levels of personal and committee staff, who are unelected and often do not require confirmation.

Many would disagree with Chayes's conclusions. Judges may appear to be more neutral by virtue of wearing the robes and taking part in the rituals of law, but most were chosen to the federal bench and the Supreme Court because of their partisanship. Any party that controls the presidency for a while will be able to "impress its political philosophy on the Court" through its judicial selections (Jackson 1997, 21). In addition, judges and justices make many decisions on the basis of their values and attitudes, rather than legal factors. If judges are consistently liberal or conservative in their decisions, that suggests they are not carefully evaluating each case on its merits, but letting their attitudes dictate their decisions. This is particularly the case for Supreme Court justices, who have reached the pinnacle of the judicial system and their careers. There are no restraints on them in their decisionmaking (Segal and Spaeth 1993). I will evaluate this more fully in Chapter 6.

The nonbureaucratic nature of judicial decisionmaking is a double-edged sword. Courts are not without their own staffs. Supreme Court justices and federal judges have recent law school graduates to assist them. However, in contrast, law clerks are transient and lack the expertise of their legislative counterparts, who make staff positions their careers. Some argue that the clerks have too much influence. Many justices leave much of their case screening, arguably their most important function, to the clerks, who often write drafts of the opinions that carry the name of the justice they serve.

Interest groups are far from absent from the deliberation in the courts. They are active in the process of selecting judges and justices. More directly, groups participate in most of the major cases of the day by means of an *amicus curiae* brief or by sponsoring litigation. As with the legislative process, some interest groups have become almost permanent fixtures in the Supreme Court and dominate an individual issue area. For instance, the American Civil Liberties Union has been a constant in First Amendment litigation, and the Legal Defense Fund of the National Association for the Advancement of Colored People dominated civil rights litigation. For decades, these groups had what amounted to control of their respective issue areas. More recently, though, the process has been thrown wide open with a proliferation of groups from all parts of the spectrum (Wasby 1995). Even if the system is skewed to a degree by the work of interest groups, a fuller range of groups is active in litigation.

While some consider the ability to tailor decisions and remedies to be a strength, others see it as a limitation on the Court. The Court faces political questions in a legal form, which, while an enormous advantage in a particular case, is seldom conducive to the systematic evaluation of policy issues. However, the fact is that the decision creates a precedent that will be applied to a myriad of other cases. In that respect, the judiciary suffers from the same problems as the legislature in painting with broad strokes without knowledge of the individual circumstances in different situations. The legislature has the advantage of having bureaucrats who can tailor the statute to the particular circumstances.

The adversarial system may better ensure that all sides will be represented in a court case, but it does not guarantee that both sides will have equal representation. In a classic study entitled "Why the 'I Haves' Come Out Ahead," Marc Galanter (1974) makes the argument that a disparity in resources and expertise often puts the parties to a particular case in very unequal positions. The haves, or Repeat Players as Galanter called them, can play the odds and bring the best cases that will create precedents favoring their views and policies. This would seem to tilt the legal system strongly in their favor. Indeed, it does in the lower courts. At the Supreme Court level, however, there are a battery of Repeat Players dedicated to protecting the views of the have-nots.

Is Capacity a Barrier?

The Constrained Court and Dynamic Court Views are ideal types that describe two ends of a spectrum, but neither is an entirely accurate portrayal of the Supreme Court's capacity and authority. The truth about the Court falls somewhere in between. Under some conditions, the Court is powerless to affect social change. In other circumstances, when the Court limits the scope of its decision or precedent and has the support of the other branches, the prospects for success are much greater.

The Constrained Court View was an accurate assessment of the Court's power at the time of the ratification of the Constitution and through the early part of American history. This was also the case after the *Dred Scott* decision and resistance to the New Deal, when the Court had placed itself in a precarious situation. Since the *Brown* decision, some would say that the Court has been closer to the Dynamic Court View, but that the Court has set itself up for failure by consistently trying to do so much.

Years of active judicial intervention in a number of issue areas, and with apparent success, led to the dominant perspective about the Court becoming the Dynamic Court View. Groups that had been shut out of the political process gained access for the first time. The justices of the Warren Court did not try to hide the fact that they were pursuing their social agendas. Lucas Powe (2000, 485) called the Warren Court "a historically unique Court operating during a historically unique era." He referred to this period as the "second American Constitutional Convention."

The institutional problems would seem to be insuperable barriers to the policymaking abilities of the Court. If the Court tries to do too much or is out of touch with the elected branches, then it is presumed that its legitimacy is in jeopardy. But look a little closer. The Court's legitimacy is considered precious coin and a finite resource. The Court has been an important branch of government for more than two centuries. It has made some very risky decisions, and still it has maintained much of its legitimacy.

To a degree, the Court can trade on its legitimacy to get some help in carrying out its policies. The Court has to choose its battles wisely. There are times when the Court needs to expend its resources, including its legitimacy. Civil rights and individual liberties seem to be worth that risk. However, it is important to remember that difficult social problems exist and no branch of government seems able to deal with some of them. In effect, though, for a number of reasons already discussed, the tie should go to the elected branches. When the branches are equally incompetent, elected officials should make the difficult judgments.

The Constrained Court View argues for judicial restraint because of the barriers that the judiciary faces. The Dynamic Court View, on the other hand, lends support to judicial activism. The special features of the judiciary not only give courts the ability to make public policy, they actually provide advantages over the other branches of government.

More specifically, the problems of implementation have led courts to develop new procedures to cope. The main problem for the Court is in following up its directives to make certain that faithful interpretation and implementation occur. The judiciary has allowed the use of certain monitoring techniques such as special masters to help gather information, overcoming one of the problems courts typically face (Rosenberg 1991, 22–26).

Rosenberg (1991, 33–35) concludes that the effectiveness of the Court in policymaking depends on the support of the political branches. The Court is able to make policy when it has the support of the other branches of government. This assistance allows the Court to overcome its institutional constraints. One of the worst problems for the Supreme Court is the failure to ensure faithful implementation. If the Court and Congress favor the same alternatives, the Court need not fear retaliation or lack of support. Public opinion is also an important resource that will help determine success.

Some would argue that the concerns with capacity may be viable, but that the Court should not necessarily bow to those pressures. Michael Perry (1982, 162) says the Court should move ahead despite problems with its capacity: "The judiciary must not forsake its prophetic function simply because its ability to secure compliance is sometimes weak, for that function is virtually indispensable when the vital, vulnerable interests of our society's marginal persons are imperiled."

Although questions of interpretation and implementation and concerns with policy outputs and impact represent an empirical dimension to the question of judicial policymaking, there is one normative and one empirical argument in favor of judicial activism. The normative notion is that Supreme Court attention to an issue, particularly one involving civil rights and individual liberties, can infuse the issue with a moral authority. The empirical dimension is this: Court attention to an issue fans public interest and may create interest and activity from the executive and legislative branches (Flemming, Bohte, and Wood 1997). It may take awhile for the other branches to react and follow the Court's lead, but eventually, they often do.

Conclusion

Under what conditions should the Supreme Court make public policy? Empirically, the question can be changed to: Under what conditions will the Supreme Court have the capacity to make effective public policy? Rosenberg summarizes two perspectives on the courts: the Constrained Court View and Dynamic Court View. These views provide a mixture of the theoretical, empirical, and practical properties of the Court. They serve as another means of evaluating the dilemma of judicial policymaking.

What about the argument that the judiciary lacks the capacity to make coherent public policy? Certainly the resolution of this issue will help analysts determine whether the courts should be active in making policy or should cede most of that responsibility to the elected branches, who presumably are more suited to the tasks. Like good attorneys presenting the evidence most favorable to their side, neither Chayes, who advocates the ability of the judiciary, nor Horowitz, who denigrates its capacities, is completely correct. The ultimate answer is not black and white. The failure of judges to ascertain certain information or foresee the possible consequences of decisions may be a function of the difficulties that all policymakers face, regardless of their institutional station.

The capacity argument is the strongest for those instances of modern judicial activism, when the Court expands its decisions to create broad-based remedies. Many of those expansive decisions come when the Court intervenes in difficult social issues. The judicial process may have significant flaws and be ineffective in dealing with intractable social problems in an absolute sense. However, many of these shortcomings are also present in the elected branches of government. As Christopher Smith (1997, 311) notes, "The criticisms directed at judicial policy making are not unique and can legitimately be aimed at other governmental policy makers as well."

Concerns for democratic theory, institutional constraints, and capacity are macrolevel issues. They go to the question of whether the Supreme Court can or should be an aggressive policymaker. Such questions ignore the microlevel, the work of individual justices. At the individual level, concerns with modern judicial activism revolve around the claim that justices are not tethered to the Constitution in making their decisions. Chapter 6 looks at the microlevel to see how individual justices make their decisions and how that contributes to understanding the dilemma of judicial policymaking.

Note

1. Under normal circumstances, a federal case begins in the District Court and then is appealed to the Court of Appeals. At that point, the case can be appealed to the Supreme Court, which has discretion over whether to accept the case. However, in major constitutional cases, like the desegregation cases, the dispute would proceed directly from the District Court to the Supreme Court.

6

The Individual
Dimension of the Dilemma:
The Bases for Decisions

Most of this book deals with the appropriate role of the Supreme Court as a policymaker. In that vein, I have discussed the Supreme Court as an institution. However, the collective decision of the Court is the result of the work of nine justices, so understanding the Court means understanding how individual justices make their decisions. When justices decide a case involving statutory or constitutional interpretation, or decide whether to invoke judicial review or overturn a precedent, they need to justify their decision. On an individual level, this provides another aspect to the debate over activism versus restraint: the grounds on which to base a decision. Notions of democratic theory and the role of the Supreme Court as the head of the judicial hierarchy raise the question of the appropriate determinants of a justice's decisions. Consider a prominent recent case as an example for this discussion.

The issue of reproductive rights is one of the classic examples of the dilemmas the Supreme Court faces as an institution. There is no reference to reproductive rights or to privacy, the right that abortion is based upon, in the Constitution. Rather, these rights were created by the Supreme Court out of whole cloth. At the state level, the elected branches had passed laws forbidding the use of contraceptives and preventing abortions. At the national level, Congress and the president had not acted. The Supreme Court ventured into this minefield and incurred the wrath of a sizable portion of the public and many members of Congress. *Roe v. Wade* (1973) was the type of decision that could have threatened the Court's legitimacy. The Court ruled that existing state laws prohibiting abortions, passed by duly constituted majorities, were unconstitutional, and that women had a qualified right to control their own reproductive decisions. The justices had no specific authority upon which to base their decision. Opponents charged that the justices were using the discredited doctrine of substantive due process, discussed in Chapter 2, to justify their decision.

Reproductive rights has been a national political issue ever since. For sixteen of the twenty years following *Roe*, Republicans dominated the White House, allowing them to place their imprint on the Supreme Court. The one Democrat to serve between 1969 and 1992, Jimmy Carter, was the only president since Reconstruction not to have the opportunity to select a Supreme Court justice.[1] During the Reagan and Bush presidencies, the abortion issue was a so-called litmus test for judicial nominees. In other words, it was the one issue that a potential nominee had to be "correct" about—in this instance, it meant opposing *Roe* and the constitutional right to have an abortion. Three of Ronald Reagan's selections, Sandra Day O'Connor, Antonin Scalia, and Anthony Kennedy, had supposedly been "right" on the issue. George Bush had the opportunity to nominate two justices, and it was assumed that David Souter and Clarence Thomas had passed the litmus test as well (Abraham 1999; Devins 1996).

Presidents Reagan and Bush also sent their solicitors general (who argue cases for the U.S. government), who typically enjoy the respect of the justices, into the Supreme Court to argue that *Roe* should be overturned. For many years, the Court refused and even strengthened *Roe*. As the liberal members of the Court retired, however, they were replaced by justices opposed to *Roe*. The numbers were mounting in favor of the right-to-life position. It was no surprise that when the Supreme Court announced that it would hear oral arguments in *Planned Parenthood of Southeastern Pennsylvania v. Casey* (1992), Court-watchers predicted the end of *Roe v. Wade*. A simple head count seemed to confirm the obvious: Chief Justice Rehnquist and Justice White had dissented from the original *Roe* decision and opposed reproductive rights from the outset. Justice Scalia joined them in opposition. Justice O'Connor, although not as militant in her opposition, frequently held that *Roe* was wrongly decided and often voted to permit state restrictions. In his first opportunity, Justice Kennedy had opposed reproductive rights also. Justices Souter and Thomas had not yet faced an abortion rights case, but they had replaced the two most liberal justices and presumably had passed the litmus test. Thus, there seemed to be at least five certain votes to overturn *Roe*.

A funny thing happened on the way to the demise of *Roe*. Justice Blackmun, the author of *Roe*, and Justice Stevens voted to uphold reproductive rights, consistent with their support of *Roe*. As expected, Rehnquist, Scalia, Thomas, and White voted to overturn the decision. The anti-*Roe* forces needed only one vote to constitute a majority. O'Connor and Kennedy were on record as opposing *Roe,* and at least one seemed certain to provide that vote. Instead, O'Connor, Kennedy, and Souter voted to sustain *Roe*.

This was curious on a number of levels. Most significantly, perhaps, there has long been an argument that Supreme Court justices consistently decide cases on the basis of their values and attitudes (Segal and Spaeth 1993). Liberals tend to vote in a liberal fashion and conservatives in a consistent conservative manner. O'Connor and Kennedy had been fairly conservative in their decisionmaking. More particularly, both had consistently supported restrictions on reproductive rights. Yet, in a case that seemed to be teed up for a reversal, they joined with Souter to protect *Roe*.

In their joint opinion, O'Connor, Kennedy, and Souter adopted judicial restraint, reaffirming *Roe* by saying that "principles of institutional integrity and the rule of *stare decisis*" (precedent) mandated the holding. Thus, the three justices put aside their values and personal preferences and supported the existing precedent because it was settled law. In their opinion, they openly discussed protecting the Court's legitimacy.

The Dilemma for the Individual Justice

The O'Connor-Kennedy-Souter opinion in *Planned Parenthood* points to the fact that even though justices make policy, there are significant differences between them and other policymakers in the executive and legislative branches. As members of the Supreme Court, justices owe a responsibility to the lower courts. They have to issue consistent decisions to create coherent doctrine for lower courts to apply, and they have to define rights and responsibilities. This may induce justices to forgo their true policy desires in favor of following precedents or ensuring consistency in doctrine. This chapter examines the individual bases of decisionmaking and how that contributes to understanding the dilemma of judicial policymaking.

Each term, the justices decide 75–150 cases, closer to the lower number in recent years. There is a great deal of controversy, both empirically and normatively, over the appropriate bases for these decisions. Here is an extreme example: What if a candidate, seeking to run for the presidency, was denied that opportunity because he was thirty-one years old? If this case got to the Supreme Court, the decision would be very easy. The Constitution states unequivocally that a candidate for the presidency has to be thirty-five years old. The clarity of this fact situation virtually guarantees that a case of this type would never make it to the Supreme Court. The lower courts would be able to resolve such a dispute.

More likely, cases that make it to the Supreme Court will fall in a much grayer area. Police need to have a warrant to search a house, but they do not need one to search an automobile. For Fourth Amendment purposes, is a mobile home a house or a car? Can a public university formulate a speech code that forbids disparaging remarks about certain groups, thus protecting civil rights, without violating the First Amendment? Can the state pay public school teachers to go into a parochial school and teach remedial courses or extracurricular classes, such as dance and music, that the Catholic school cannot afford without violating the separation of church and state under the First Amendment? None of those issues could have possibly been foreseen by the framers of the Constitution. This poses a problem for those who want the justices to use the Constitution as the sole or major determinant of their decisions.

Even issues that reappear or raise recurrent questions—such as the propriety of the death penalty, the constitutional protection enjoyed by the print media, and defendants' rights—require the justices to interpret cryptic provisions of the Constitution or the Bill of Rights. These issues raise a number of questions. If the Constitution is vague, what are the appropriate means of inferring its meaning? Does the Constitution change with the times? Does the First Amendment or the definition of cruel and unusual punishment mean something different today than it meant in 1805 or in 1920? It raises other questions as well. What should guide the justices if the text of the Constitution does not provide the answer and the intent of the framers is unclear? Justices will be making decisions that have major policy consequences. How can they ground those decisions?

The ideal view of the justices portrays them as carefully weighing the arguments of both sides, consulting the constitutional provision or statute in question, trying to understand the intent of the framers, and trying to square the case with existing precedents. Some refer to the ideal form of decisionmaking as mechanical jurisprudence; that, coupled with the supposed nonpolitical nature of the judiciary, made it easy to separate the courts from the rest of the government conceptually. The justices have long contributed to the notion that politics and law can be separated (Fisher 1988, 9–16).

The reality, according to some political scientists, is that justices are completely free to follow their own designs in deciding cases. Constitutional provisions are vague, statutory language provides little guidance, and there are a number of conflicting precedents that could be brought to bear in most cases. This frees the individual justice to look elsewhere for a reason for the decision. There are other aspects that expand the discretion of justices. They have lifetime tenure in a position that is at the pinnacle of the judicial system. They do not have to modify their behavior to keep their positions or earn a promotion. Empirically, studies show that justices act very consistently in their decisionmaking. The selection process encourages presidents to nominate jurists who will reflect their views on the issues (Baum 1997).

The argument that justices decide cases on the basis of their preferences got very visible support from the *Bush v. Gore* (2000) case. This stemmed from the fact that the five most conservative justices ignored their traditional deference to state courts to support the arguments made by the attorneys for Bush. The four most liberal justices, on the other hand, supported the position advocated by the Gore legal team.

Still, despite the evidence that justices are consistent in their decisionmaking and that presidents spend a great deal of time screening potential nominees to get one who reflects their views, members of the Court do not admit the influence of their values and attitudes. Nominees steadfastly maintain that they will follow the normative civics book ideal: They will weigh the facts in the case, look to the framers, and consider the relevant precedents, and only then will they make a decision. The veil of secrecy that surrounds the Court gives the justices a great deal of discretion. Their legitimacy is protected if they do not abuse that freedom. *Bush v. Gore* removed that veil, if only for a brief time. What is left to restrain justices and keep them from merely following their policy goals? Some argue that it is only individual self-restraint that keeps justices from acting as superlegislators and from merely following their policy goals. The symbols of the Supreme Court, the marble palace and robes, as well as the law, are powerful restraints, but they may or may not serve as a counterforce to the freedom and job security that justices enjoy.

Do justices simply act on their sincere preferences, or are they restrained by legal factors? As always, the truth is somewhere in the middle. Justices have a great deal of leeway and often follow their own views in making decisions. In many cases and on a number of issues, though, justices follow clear precedents, defer to the elected branches, or support a well-developed interpretation of a constitutional provision. Despite certain ideological divisions on the Court, a large percentage of the cases are decided unanimously, meaning that warring justices agree in a number of circumstances (Pacelle 1991, 85–87).

When a Supreme Court justice faces an issue with major policy consequences, on what bases does the individual justice decide the case and choose between competing arguments? That question is the focus of this chapter. I will start by considering some examples. During the beginning of the hostilities that would become known as World War II, a school board suspended a number of students who refused to salute the flag because they felt that violated their religious beliefs. In *Minersville School District v. Gobitis* (1940), the Supreme Court had to decide whether the suspension was justified. Justice Felix Frankfurter, who was a member of what he called a persecuted class, Jews, was sympathetic to their claims, but he argued that he could not interfere with the school board's directive. Frankfurter reasoned that he was unelected and therefore in no position to substitute his judgment for that of the school board (Bartee 1984, 68).[2]

For almost two decades, women and their doctors in Connecticut had challenged a state ban on birth control. Until 1965, the Supreme Court refused to entertain such cases, arguing that the doctors did not have standing to challenge the law on behalf of their patients. A number of justices, led by William Douglas, felt that laws banning the use of contraceptive devices were fundamentally wrong and violated an individual's right to privacy. Despite the fact that he and his colleagues were not elected, he felt no reservations about saying that the state law should be struck down. However, the Constitution makes no explicit provisions for privacy. The justices who wanted to reach this result needed to "invent" constitutional provisions to support their arguments. Douglas reasoned in *Griswold v. Connecticut* (1965) that freedom of association rights under the First Amendment, freedom for the homeowner from the forcible quartering of troops under the Third Amendment and from illegal search and seizure under the Fourth Amendment, and due process under the Fifth Amendment all suggested the framers' concern with privacy.[3] Douglas argued that taken together, these provisions suggested the existence of a constitutionally based right to privacy. Further, he claimed that privacy was a fundamental right that could not be abridged unless the state demonstrated a compelling reason.

The right to privacy, despite its shaky constitutional foundation, became the basis for the right to an abortion. Once again, a Court majority argued that state laws, passed by elected officials, which forbid women from terminating their pregnancies, were unconstitutional. In *Planned Parenthood*, Justices O'Connor, Kennedy, and Souter, who had expressed reservations about *Roe*, voted to uphold it. In language that was a textbook example of judicial restraint, the three argued that the law was settled and mere politics should not be the impetus for changing it.

These are but three of the more than 5,000 decisions the Supreme Court has issued since 1940. They are not representative of the Court's work, but they present a snapshot of some of the roles the Court can play in American politics and some of the factors that lead justices to their decisions. Frankfurter and the *Casey* trio of justices showed different forms of judicial restraint. The latter followed precedent, while the former cited deference to the elected branches. Douglas, on the other hand, offered a triple dose of judicial activism: willing to accept a case that had jurisdictional defects, anxious to overturn the work of the elected branches, and creative enough to construct new constitutional rights.

As discussed, there is a great deal of controversy over the appropriate role of the Court. At one end of the continuum, some argue that the Court should proceed slowly and defer to the elected branches of government. They would have the Court play an interstitial role and "interpret" the law, rather than "make" it. At the other end of the spectrum, proponents of sweeping judicial power want the Court to assume its place as a coequal branch of government. They are not troubled by the fact that justices may need to "make" law or legislate from the bench. They are not reluctant to substitute the Court's collective judgment for that of Congress or the president. Of course, there are a whole range of alternatives between these extremes.

Judicial decisions are categorized as following a political or a legal model. The political model of judicial policymaking means that justices adopt positions that

Figure 6.1   With Just the Right Light, Justice Douglas "finds" the right to privacy. Cartoon by Laura Gunther.

reflect their conceptions of desirable public policy. These justices would try to use the cases before them to advance their policy goals. Theoretically, the opposite view is that justices adopt legal decisionmaking methods. Justices would follow the dictates of the law, the Constitution, and precedent in order to establish predictability and consistency in the law to guide the lower courts. Law-oriented justices would put aside their policy views to fulfill their obligations to the lower courts.

The public is not privy to what happens in the Supreme Court. The justices enter the courtroom in the Supreme Court building in long black robes, emerging from behind a curtain. They toil away, relatively invisible, their faces and names unknown to most Americans. Cameras are not allowed in the courtroom to record oral arguments. No one is allowed in the conference room except the justices when they are in deliberations. It is relatively easy to hide the influence of political factors and to maintain what many argue is the illusion that justices are disinterested actors paying attention strictly to legal factors. *Bush v. Gore* was different. Minutes after the oral arguments concluded, a tape of the proceedings was made available and aired nationally. The public got a peek beneath the judicial robes and a sense of who the justices are and what they do.

Are judges policymakers? The bottom line for many is the question of whether judges make the law or find the law. Is the judge like a referee who only applies the rules that others have written? Or is the judge a lawmaker rather than merely an interpreter of the law? In one sense, every decision reflects policymaking. Any time the Court makes a choice between two litigants and between two competing justifications, it makes policy on at least a limited basis. The question then is not whether justices make policy, it is a question of how much policy they make.

In a famous quote, Jeremiah Smith, a state judge, remarked "Do judges make law? Course they do. Made some myself." Judge Jerome Frank claimed that "All judges exercise discretion, individualize abstract laws, make law" (O'Brien 1997, 136). As one moves up the judicial hierarchy toward the Supreme Court, the elements of judicial policymaking become more pronounced. According to David O'Brien (1997, 137), "In a system based on a written Constitution and with an independent judiciary, constitutional interpretation is necessary, judicial creativity important, and judicial lawmaking to some degree inevitable."

Every decision that a Supreme Court justice makes is inherently political. The Court hears a small number of cases, focusing on the most important issues of the times. Accepting that the Court's decisions are political and have important policy consequences does not explain how those decisions were made. As Frankfurter claimed, "Constitutional law is at all not a science, but applied politics" (O'Brien 1997, 137). To at least some degree, justices are making law and making policy. Judicial restraint would minimize the amount of policymaking.

How do Supreme Court justices make the individual decisions that lead to a Court opinion? On the most basic grounds, there are two sets of factors or determinants that justices consider when they weigh the alternatives in a case: legal and extralegal. These are sometimes referred to by the unwieldy terms *interpretivism* and *non-interpretivism*, respectively. Table 6.1 shows the legal and extralegal factors justices typically use in making their decisions. Suffice it to say that on normative grounds, the legal factors are considered preferable to the extralegal. Proponents of judicial restraint say that interpretivism is a process of law while non-interpretivism is a process of politics (McKeever 1993, 29).

The terms *legal* and *extralegal* refer to a variety of modes of judicial interpretation. The legal factors represent a number of approaches that suggest that justices do their utmost to put their policy views, prejudices, and biases aside when they confront an issue, and decide cases by referring to factors that have a grounding in the law. The legal model argues that judges do not have great discretion in deciding cases. A number of analysts reject this formulaic perception of mechanical jurisprudence. The so-called legal realists[4] have refuted the idea that judges lack such discretion, arguing, in effect, that judges make law. Extralegal factors, on the

TABLE 6.1 Individual Determinants of Supreme Court Decisionmaking

Legal Determinants	Extralegal Determinants
Intent of the framers of the Constitution	Individual values and attitudes
Intent of the framers of statute	Sincere policy preferences
Meaning of the words: Constitution	Strategic decisionmaking
Meaning of the words: Statutes	
Logical reasoning	
Neutral principles	
Precedent	

Source: Richard Pacelle.

other hand, allow the justices to include political considerations in their calculations and to use their ideological views to inform their decisions. While the legal factors may be the desirable ones, it is clear that extralegal factors may be a better practical explanation for judicial decisionmaking. On the simplest, most general level, the differences between legal and extralegal are reflected in the differences between finding the law and making the law.

Legal Factors in Decisionmaking

Legal factors represent a variety of different approaches that ask the justices to consult the Constitution, statutes, and precedents. As noted, these approaches are sometimes referred to as interpretivism. In a sense, they ask the justices to find the law and suggest where they might find it. The most dominant legal factors are the intent of the Constitution's framers, the meaning of the words, logical reasoning, neutral principles, and precedent. Perhaps the best known of the legal factors suggests that justices should consult the original intent of the framers of the Constitution or the intent of the legislators in passing a law. Justices are asked to construe the statutes or constitutional provisions according to the preferences of those who originally drafted and supported them (Spaeth 1995, 300). When the justices face a question that involves the Constitution, the central charter of American government, they need to try to understand what the framers meant by the provision in question. The framers chose their language deliberately as a guide to future generations. Using original intent fosters stability in the law and grounds decisions in the Constitution, rather than leaving them to the values of the justices.

Using the intent of the framers is consistent with judicial restraint. Restraintists feel bound to search for some kind of meaning in the Constitution. Justices who subscribe to restraint would search for the intent of the framers and adapt it pragmatically to the current context. Justices can infer powers and rights from the structures and relationships created by the Constitution (McKeever 1993, 30–31). The intent of the framers provides some black-letter constitutional principles for future justices and lower court judges to follow, and produces neutral principles of law that can be applied to similar cases. Thus, using intent takes the broad discretion out of the hands of unelected justices.

The justices can attempt to use the specific language of the Constitution to inform their decisions. This would seem to represent value-free jurisprudence, as the justices use the literal meaning of the words of the document's provisions to guide their decisions rather than their personal views. If justices do not want to rely on the specific language, they can attempt to glean the meaning of the words at the time the framers authored them. Thus, the words of the Constitution define the extent and limits of power. As with the other modes of interpretation, this will, in theory, create consistency and predictability in the law (Epstein and Walker 1998a, 28–29).

If the Constitution is not clear or the case represents an issue the framers could not have foreseen, this creates problems for the justices. In such instances, how would the justices develop standards for their decisions that do not leave them to their own unconstrained policy views? Justices can rely on two legal factors: logical reasoning, which is bounded by the Constitution, and neutral principles, which allow them to consider some external values consistent with the Constitution. *Marbury v. Madison* is a classic example of logical reasoning. Chief Justice Marshall assumed that because the framers created the Supreme Court, they must have meant to give it the power of judicial review. In *McCulloch v. Maryland*, Marshall reasoned that if Congress had the authority to tax and coin money, it should have the power to establish a national bank (Epstein and Walker 1998a, 143–149).

Many theorists argue that there are a set of fundamental values and neutral principles that can be inferred from the overall provisions and intent of the Constitution. For example, analysts might say that when faced with questions, justices should err on the side of promoting democratic values. Justices who try to ground their decisions on broader principles that go beyond their personal views might seek a philosophy based on the general notions tied to the Constitution rather than explicit provisions of the document. Some justices treat the Constitution as a document of aspiration, containing moral principles to endure for ages (Goldstein 1995, 276).

In interpreting the Constitution, Archibald Cox (1976, 114) argued that the justices need to discern "principles sufficiently absolute to give them roots throughout the community and continuity over significant periods of time, and to lift them above the level of the pragmatic political judgments of a particular time and place." The Constitution is supposed to provide the justices with enduring principles, even if there are not specific answers to the particular case. In addition, the decisions of the justices are more legitimate if they follow a principled process of discovering and enunciating the shared enduring values of society (Bickel 1962, 58).

These legal factors would hold for statutory as well as constitutional construction. Justices evaluating a statutory provision would use the intent of the framers of the legislation and the meaning of the words of the statute, deferring to the elected legislators who passed the statute. The justices are also governed by rules that require deference to the governmental agencies and administrators that have to implement the statutory provisions.

The final legal factor is precedent, the doctrine of *stare decisis*. Under this doctrine, judges are to be governed by similar previous decisions. When a case comes to the Supreme Court, justices should seek relevant precedents and apply them to the situation at hand. Following precedent creates stability and introduces predictability to the law. According to Harlan Fiske Stone, "The rule of *stare decisis* embodies a wise policy because it is often more important that a rule of law be settled than that it be settled right" (Epstein and Walker 1998b, 27). Lower court justices will know what is expected of them and citizens will know the extent of their rights if the law is consistent.

The doctrine of stare decisis takes the decision away from the justices and provides the necessary direction for lower court judges when they have to apply the principles to similar cases. Everyone in the legal system understands the importance of precedents. In arguing cases, lawyers raise the precedents most favorable to their side. In deciding cases, justices cite the precedents most relevant to their decisions. According to Sheldon Goldman, "the rule of precedent symbolizes that we are dealing with a court of law as distinguished from a legislative body" (Epstein and Walker 1998a, 21).

Legal factors try to remove politics from the decision and suggest that the law can be found, whether in precedents, the language of the statute or Constitution, or in the intent of the authors of their provisions. The decisions are supposed to be principled. As Stephen Wasby (1984, 208–209) notes, "Compromises derived from pragmatism are for legislators and political executives; courts, on the other hand, must stand for principle, deliberateness, the use of rationality and logic, and detachment from the turmoil and passion of political conflict."

The importance of the legal factors is reflected in all of the trappings and symbols of the judicial system. The statue of Thebes, the representation of justice, is blindfolded to suggest that no one will be prejudged. On the other hand, if judges are left to their own devices to make decisions that are not tied to the Constitution or past decisions, then it introduces instability into the law. If justices make the decisions without a grounding in the legal factors, then law and the interpretation of the Constitution would change with the composition of the Court and with the shifting winds of politics.

Problems with the Legal Factors

While normative theory supports the use of legal factors, such factors are not without problems. First, some analysts argue that justices use their values and attitudes and extralegal factors to make decisions, and then claim to have used one of the legal factors. The legal factor, then, becomes a legitimate cover for a decision that might be based on less legitimate factors. Second, the legal factors are not as clear or universally accepted as one might think.

Those who believe justices rely on extralegal factors claim that justices determine how they want to decide the case and use original intent as justification. In other words, they use the intent of the framers to cover their personal designs. If justices want to use a broad interpretation of the Constitution that keeps up with the times, they pay less attention to the intent of the framers. Others may opt for a narrow interpretation and closer adherence to the original intent of the framers (Baum 2001, 141). As Harold Spaeth notes (1995, 300–301), it is not uncommon for justices in both the majority and in dissenting opinions in the same case to refer to the intent of the framers to support their conflicting views.

The idea that the justices should rely on the intent of the framers, precedents, and neutral, shared principles presupposes that such legal factors are readily identifiable and applicable to novel fact situations. That is not necessarily the case. For instance, when the justices look to the intent of the framers of the Constitution, which framers should they consult? There were many men who could be considered framers. Besides those who signed the document, there were others who took part but left Philadelphia (Spaeth 1995, 300). In addition, there was a great deal of controversy over a number of provisions of the Constitution before the document was completed. Some of the framers supported stronger central government, while others did not. There were differences in how much authority the framers wanted to give Congress and the president. The framers hid their differences under "cloaks of generality" (Eisler 1993, 268). Whose interpretation should dominate in those circumstances? There is also concern with how clear and accurate the records of the time are. Inferring intent from such records, even if they are clear, is a difficult enterprise.

As a result of these concerns, some maintain the search for original intent is impossible. Justice Brennan called the search "arrogance cloaked in humility" (Eisler 1993, 268). William Howard Taft, who served as president and later chief justice, claimed that the argument that the "judges should interpret the exact intention of those who established the Constitution was a theory of one who does not understand the proper administration of justice" (O'Brien 1997, 135).

The question of the intent of a statute is even more troublesome. The search for statutory intent can be found in committee reports and debates on the floor of the House and Senate. Members of Congress can insert comments into the *Congressional Record* or edit their submissions after the fact. How could one infer the intent of legislators from that variety of sources? The legislative process is fraught with veto points. As a result, laws are typically vague and open-ended, leaving a great deal of room for inferring intent. Often, the evidence of legislative intent can be conflicting. Sometimes that is deliberate, as different members of Congress, even those opposing the legislation, try to influence the justices in what they assume will be an inevitable court challenge (Baum 2001, 141). In addition, there are scores of legislators involved in passage, and they are likely to have a number of motives for supporting the legislation in question. The justices may decide to ignore intent when it violates their policy goals. Despite clear legislative intent in the Civil Rights Act of 1964 that forbade affirmative action, the Supreme Court willingly supported the policy (Spaeth 1995, 300–301).

Precedent is difficult to use as a guide as well. Precedents usually exist on both sides. Both litigants in the case cite a number of precedents, and the opinion of the Court, as well as any concurring and dissenting opinions, will cite a score of precedents. If precedents truly governed, then few cases would get through the judicial hierarchy. They would be decided in the lower courts with little discretion needed because previous decisions would be controlling. Spaeth (1995, 303) believes that precedent is only a matter of style rather than a substantive limitation on judges.

Few cases before the Supreme Court are governed by clear precedents. In most instances, the case before the Court is different from the existing precedent (Baum 2001, 142). That can free the justices to use their own values to make the decision. Justices can appear to follow a precedent even when they are circumventing it. They can distinguish a present case from an existing precedent, holding that the precedent is not overturned, but that it does not apply in the particular circumstance. The justices can also narrow the reach of the precedent without overturning it. In criminal procedure, the Burger and Rehnquist Courts created a number of exceptions to the exclusionary rule and *Miranda* rights, without overturning the major precedents, *Mapp v. Ohio* or *Miranda v. Arizona*. Similarly, in reproductive rights, *Roe* remains precedent, but it is a shell of its original strength. The Court has riddled it with exceptions and qualifications.

The literal or plain meaning of the words would seem, on the face of it, to create the fewest problems. However, words tend to have a variety of meanings, and when that occurs, which particular one should be used? Harold Spaeth (1995, 299) uses the example of the *Sullivan v. Stroop* case. The author of the majority opinion used the *Random House Dictionary*, while the dissenters utilized *Black's Law Dictionary*. In some instances, the justices reject the clear meaning of the words. The Marshall Court, which was working within a reasonable proximity of the framing of the Constitution, defined *citizens* to include corporations (Newmyer 1968). The justices changed the meaning of the Fourteenth Amendment a number of times. Within a decade of its passage, the Court took away the protection for the freed slaves, the primary rationale for its existence (Epstein and Walker 1998b, 640).

Most of the cases that the justices are asked to resolve do not lend themselves to the plain meaning of the words. The First Amendment reads that "Congress shall make no law . . ." limiting freedom of speech, association, or religion. Except for Hugo Black, no justices read the First Amendment in this absolute fashion.[5] The justices even disagree as to the meaning of "speech" in the First Amendment: For some, it means only the spoken word, while others feel it involves a broader range of activities, including forms of nonverbal expression such as burning a flag. The Fifth and Fourteenth Amendments involve "due process" of the law. What does that mean when it is applied to specific circumstances? Federal statutes often do not provide a great deal of guidance either, meaning that the plain meaning of the words may not be sufficient for the justices.

Failing to determine the clear meaning of the words or the intent of the framers, justices would be urged by proponents of legal factors to pay attention to a series of neutral principles that are based on the broader philosophical goals of the Constitution. Justices may develop or advocate a constitutional theory or philosophy, which serves as a framework of principles that guide them in deciding constitutional questions. The problem is that some portion of those philosophies fall outside the text of the Constitution. While many can agree on the broader notions of protecting democratic values and encouraging full participation, there is no consensus on the specifics and how they relate to individual cases, thus inviting the justices to substitute their own values for the broader principles that should direct decisionmaking (Goldstein 1995, 286–289).

All justices cite precedents in their decisions. Most justices try to stick to the meaning of provisions of the Constitution and attempt to infer the intent of the framers of the Constitution and statutes. But how important are those factors? Do justices use those factors to come to a decision after weighing the facts and the law? Or do they reach a conclusion based on their personal values and then look for "legitimate" justifications for their decisions? A look at the extralegal factors may shed some light on these questions.

Extralegal Factors in Decisionmaking

If justices always followed relevant precedents or original intent or always deferred to legislators or agencies, it would not matter a great deal who a president selected when there was a vacancy on the Supreme Court. If justices were entirely neutral, then presidents would make their selections purely on the basis of the expertise and experience of prospective nominees. The policy views of the possible nominees would not come into play. Whether a nominee is liberal or conservative would be irrelevant given that justices would use legal factors to make their decisions.

All the evidence suggests that it makes a difference who the president selects. Presidents and their advisors spend a great deal of time screening possible candidates for the bench. Extralegal factors play an important role in judicial decisionmaking. Some refer to extralegal factors by the term *non-interpretivism.* Extralegal factors, or non-interpretivism, refer to political or personal approaches to decisionmaking. Some maintain it leads to justices making the law rather than finding it.

Presidents claim that they want a justice who will interpret the law rather than make the law. Justices do not admit that they use their values and attitudes or extralegal factors in decisionmaking. They will, on occasion, accuse other justices they disagree with of using their policy preferences in deciding cases (Spaeth 1995, 306).

Many argue that in making decisions, non-interpretivist justices do not pay serious attention to the Constitution or the intent of the framers. Rather, these justices make individual decisions on the basis of their policy goals, ideological predilections, and individual preferences. They use precedents and constitutional provisions to provide justification for those decisions (McKeever 1993, 30–31). Studies show that justices are very consistent in their decisionmaking over time. Justices who were liberal (or conservative) before they came to the Court tend to decide cases consistent with their predispositions. When presidents nominate justices, then, they try to find someone who will reflect their policy views.

The fact that justices are free to make their decisions on whatever grounds they choose is considered troubling on normative grounds. Justices who are not elected and have lifetime tenure can make constitutional decisions that are effectively final and cannot be overturned by the voters or the elected branches. Once on the Court and freed from political restraints, justices are able to act purely on their beliefs. If values and attitudes are as important as many analysts believe, then the justices are close to being completely unfettered in decisionmaking. There is little accountability or responsibility. If the justices do not tie their decisions to existing precedents, the language of the Constitution, or the intent of the framers, then they are, in effect, becoming "superlegislators" who do not have to face the voters.

Jeffrey Segal and Harold Spaeth are the primary proponents of the idea that the justices are motivated almost exclusively by their attitudes and values. Lower court judges need to pay attention to precedent and legal factors in hopes of being promoted to a higher court and to avoid being reversed by a higher court. Once justices reach the Supreme Court, however, they have achieved the pinnacle of their careers. They are free to vote their policy views with few consequences. They cannot be removed from office and their constitutional decisions can only be reversed by extraordinary majorities. The only restraints on them are self-imposed.

Empirically, it is clear that the attitudes and values of the justices are very important determinants of their decisionmaking. The results of analyses are too consistent to deny the influence of the policy views of the justices. Is this a modern phenomenon or has it existed since the beginning of the Court? Prior to the 1930s, the overwhelming majority of the Court's decisions were unanimous. Despite the issue, the justices agreed on the decisions. Part of this may have been a function of the fact that the justices had to accept every case brought to them before 1925. Thus, there were many noncontroversial cases on the docket. Others say that the norms of consensus on the Court have broken down over time, leading to more non-unanimous decisions and to more non-interpretivism (Walker, Epstein, and Dixon 1988).

It has been the case that even though non-interpretivism may be much closer to empirical reality, the legal model is held up as the paragon of the way things should be. More recently, some of those who advocate, or at least accept, the reality of non-interpretivism have argued that interpretivism and legal factors have become irrelevant. They view interpretivism as a remnant of a bygone era, claiming non-interpretivism better serves contemporary policy needs. These proponents argue that social and moral issues are difficult, and the unelected federal judiciary is the best institution to address them (McKeever 1993, 46). They also believe that it is appropriate for the justices, who were chosen by an elected president and confirmed by an elected Senate, to use their values and attitudes to make their decisions.

Relying on the Constitution: Legal or Extralegal?

When he served on the Supreme Court, Justice Black always carried a well-worn copy of the Constitution in his pocket, which he could consult during conferences with his brethren. Many critics of the modern Court charge that some justices have lost sight of the Constitution and instead make decisions based on their policy views. Wolfe (1997) argues that this modern form of judicial activism has loosened justices from the moorings of the Constitution. Reliance on the Constitution is often assumed to be a component of the legal model. But as with most of the generalizations in this book, it is a little more complicated. There has long been the argument that interpretation of a statute or the Constitution is law, not politics. When justices rest their decision on the provisions of a statute or the Constitution, then it appears they are using legal factors. It is not that simple. The Constitution and most statutes have vague provisions. The interpretation of those provisions is seldom self-evident and may involve extralegal considerations and the policy views of the justices.

If the Constitution is to be the foundation of decisionmaking, particularly under the legal model, then one of the most basic questions to be asked is, What exactly constitutes the Constitution? This seems to be a ridiculous question: The Constitution is a well-known document that sits in the federal archives and is included in every American politics textbook. Some justices and many commentators feel that this is the Constitution, period. That is referred to as textualism. Others take the broader view that the Constitution includes the intent of the framers, *The Federalist Papers,* and the broad, enduring notions that have guided the construction of the nation. Those who argue that there is more to the Constitution than the document itself claim that the Constitution can only be understood as a product of the political theories that helped spawn the document. In any event, this broader view of the Constitution, referred to as extratextualism, invites justices to bring other factors into their decision calculus.

Unpeeling another layer reveals related questions. Does the Constitution change with the times? Are its provisions static or dynamic? Some argue the framers established a document with a fixed meaning. Chief Justice Taney believed the Constitution "speaks not only in the same words, but with the meaning and intent with which it spoke when it came from the hands of its framers. . . . Any other rule of construction would abrogate the judicial character of this Court, and make it mere reflex of popular opinion or passion of the day" (O'Brien 1997, 135). The problem, of course, is that the argument that the Constitution changes with the times can be used as an excuse for allowing the justices to impose their own views and positions on the cases they decide. This was troubling to Justice Black who argued that unbounded judicial creativity and license "would make of this Court's members a day-to-day constitutional convention" (O'Brien, 1997, 136).

Others support the view of a living Constitution. Even John Marshall seemed to suggest that when he wrote, "We must never forget this is a Constitution we are expounding . . . intended to endure for ages to come and, consequently, to be adapted to the various crises of human affairs." Changing political circumstances present novel issues that are not covered by the text of the document. New conditions arise that the framers could not have foreseen, such as technological developments or the changes that history has wrought. This leaves discretion for the justices. As Murphy, Fleming, and Harris (1986, 127) noted, "As conditions have changed, so have political institutions, ideas, and ideals."

Those who believe that the Constitution is more than the document typically support the notion of a changing or living Constitution. As Murphy, Fleming, and Harris (1986, 128) wrote, "Those who accept current authority to adapt the Constitution commonly see 'the Constitution' as including much more than the document, though some may view the Ninth and Fourteenth Amendments as windows that let in a wider world." While the notion of a dynamic Constitution is more amenable to judicial activism, those who support judicial restraint could also accept the view that the Constitution changes with the times. Judicial restraintists would try to find some constitutional theory or enduring principles to use as a guide, rather than let their values dictate their decisions (Rehnquist 1997, 143–144). Judicial activists who believe the Constitution changes with the times might use their values and beliefs as the basis for deciding how the Constitution has changed.

Procedurally, even those justices who want to utilize the Constitution faithfully must conduct a historical inquiry into the origins of the relevant clauses to ascertain their meaning. Those justices rely primarily on the words and clauses of the document. If that is not enough of a guide, they look to the underlying intent of the framers. Proponents of restraint argue that only by these methods can the inherently undemocratic nature of judicial review be brought into line with the principles of democratic theory. But, in reality, can that be done?

More likely, most justices attach their personal values and their own constitutional theories to their interpretation of the Constitution. Though the decisions seem to be grounded in the Constitution, there is still a level of abstraction that amounts to extratextualism. When they interpret the history of the provisions or intuit the meaning of the framers, the justices insert some of their own perceptions and biases. What this has created, in effect, is an ongoing informal system of constitutional politics. This represents an informal process of constitutional amendment that occurs when the justices render interpretation of the Constitution (Goldstein 1995, 281–289). They do not change the Constitution, but they modify the interpretation of it and create a precedent that their successors are theoretically obligated to follow.

Reconciling the Two Perspectives

At the individual level, justices face one of the classic dilemmas of American politics. The Supreme Court, as a collectivity, and the justices, as individuals, work at the intersection between law and policy, between the legal and political realms. Justices have complicated jobs and try to achieve a number of different goals. As a result, explaining decisionmaking is more complicated than either the pure legal model or the pure extralegal model maintains.

Justices are motivated by a variety of goals: some legal, some policy-oriented. By virtue of their training and socialization in law school and throughout their years as attorneys and lower court judges, justices are taught respect for the law and precedent. According to Lawrence Baum (1997, 17), legal goals can include the desire for an accurate interpretation of the law and legal clarity and consistency. The justices take their responsibilities as the apex of the judicial hierarchy seriously. They have to introduce stability and predictability to the law. Thus, they have to adhere to precedent and set guidelines for the lower courts to follow. At the same time, most of the issues that come before the Court reflect the significant questions of the day. There is no doubt that the individual policy goals and the desire to achieve good policy outcomes are important and maybe most important in most cases. However, they are not the sole determinant in every case.

It is hard to ignore the evidence that justices rely on extralegal factors. First, they have the freedom to do so, by virtue of the fact that they serve for life and are unelected. Second, justices do not need to impress anyone to continue their personal voyages. As far as the judicial system is concerned, justices are at the peak of their profession. Although one justice, Charles Evans Hughes, left the Court to run for the presidency,[6] most will end their professional lives when they leave the High Court. Third, justices demonstrate a great deal of consistency in their decisionmaking over time.

Proponents of the legal model would counter that all justices cite precedent and all use justifications based on the words and meaning of the Constitution (or statute) or the intent of the framers. Litigants and groups who file briefs and argue the cases cite precedents, base their positions on constitutional and statutory provisions, and often argue about the intent of the framers. However, is the use of these legal factors a shroud or veil that the justices place over the use of extralegal factors? Does a conservative justice wanting to make an ideological decision invoke original intent when it supports that decision? Or is the use of intent the reason for the decision? Does a liberal justice rely on precedent because his or her ideological views are supported by the existing precedent? Or is that precedent accepted because it is better that the law is settled and consistent?

A human face can be put on the analysis by asking more questions. Was Felix Frankfurter merely a conservative justice who hid behind the legal factors? Or was he, as he claimed, a liberal who had to put his personal beliefs aside in favor of precedent, deference to the elected branches, and a faithfulness to statutory and constitutional language? Even if it is true that the very liberal and very conservative justices are acting on their values and attitudes, what motivates the justices who are in the middle? Why are justices such as O'Connor and Lewis Powell, who occupied the moderate positions, the least likely to vote to overturn a precedent?

It is difficult to answer these questions, but justices use a combination of legal and extralegal factors when they make their individual decisions. Based on the evidence, it appears that values and attitudes dominate decisionmaking in many issue areas. It is also clear, however, that all justices rely on legal factors in at least some cases. The justices may desire to use their values and attitudes to guide their decisions, but in cases with clear precedents they may be constrained by previous decisions. In some percentage of cases each term, the Court's decisions are unanimous. It does seem that the moderate justices adopt the position that will protect the institution and avoid overturning past precedents, as O'Connor, Kennedy, and Souter did in the *Planned Parenthood* decision.

There are theories that seem to combine some of the legal and attitudinal models. One holds that the justices have a bifurcated agenda. There are issues that the justices care about deeply and, as such, they use their values and attitudes to make decisions in those areas. Then there are cases that are not central to the concerns of individual justices and so they follow precedent. Certain issue areas, for the most part in the economic realm, do not seem to elicit policy responses from the justices. Cases in those areas may be accepted because there is a lower court conflict or because the Court feels that there is an institutional obligation to settle the dispute. Those decisions are often narrow and unanimous, suggesting that legal factors are overcoming extralegal considerations (Pacelle 1991, 80–84; Perry 1991, 277–282).

Others analysts, most notably Lee Epstein and Jack Knight (1998, 10–13), claim that the values and attitudes of the justices are a starting point, but justices are constrained and unable to act completely on those values. Epstein and Knight believe that, left to their own devices, justices would base their decisions on their sincere preferences. The Court does face some important constraints, particularly in cases involving statutory interpretation, and the justices must respect those in making decisions. Congress can overturn statutory decisions by a simple majority, so the Court adjusts its preferred outcome to get closer to a point Congress will find acceptable.

Thus, justices act strategically, taking into account the elected branches, their colleagues on the Court, or public opinion. In doing so, the justices will blunt opposition and protect the institution's legitimacy. In considering and deferring to the elected branches or following precedent, the justices may move a little closer to the legal end of the continuum. In constitutional interpretation, however, the justices have fewer constraints on their decisions and may be closer to the political end of the political-legal spectrum. Even then, the justices may show restraint and refuse to overturn precedents.

Conclusion

Justice Thomas has said, "I just follow the law, so it does not make any difference what my opinions are" (Baum 2001, 138). All nominees tell the Senate Judiciary Committee the same thing, but that view does not reflect reality. The justices have always made political decisions. They have always used precedent as well as provisions of the Constitution and statutes. There has always been a mixture of the legal and extralegal determinants of decisionmaking. Historically, there had been a long tradition of ignoring precedent that supported extratextual decisions. While history has given us examples of judicial activism and overt policymaking over time, there is a sense that the two have become more prevalent in the last half-century. Indeed, analysts have labeled this modern judicial activism.

Traditionally, people assumed that the normative ideal for judicial decisionmaking was a reflection of reality. Judges and justices were seen as disinterested and above politics. With this myth intact, the decisions of the Court gained a great deal of legitimacy and respect. When the so-called legal realists stripped away the veneer that hid the true determinants of decisionmaking, some of the normative cover for the justices was gone.

Studies demonstrate that ideologies, as reflected in the values and attitudes of the justices, are the dominant factors in decisionmaking. To some analysts, even the use of legal factors is colored by the influence of ideology and individual values. Many argue that texts are indeterminant and cannot constrain judges. The justices ordinarily decide cases that involve "ambiguous applications of the Constitution or federal statutes—cases in which the proper interpretation of the law is far from clear" (Baum 2001, 139). This ambiguity provides justices who are so inclined with the leeway to use their values and attitudes to guide their decisions.

Even the use of original intent seems to argue for some extratextualism (Goldstein 1995, 280).

Justices use open-ended provisions of the Constitution as well as words such as *justice* and *equal* as anchors for the vague language of the Constitution to give them a grounding in the legal factors (Goldstein 1995, 281). Some claim that when justices are forced to define *justice* and *equal* and *due process,* the definition stems from their individual values and policy goals.

Yet, having said all that, it would be a mistake to dismiss the existence of legal factors or to accept the view that values and attitudes are the sole determinant of decisionmaking. First, there are a number of unanimous decisions each term. Second, in some issue areas, the desire to impose stability on the law is more important than the direction of the decision. Finally, in a number of areas, even though a clear majority of the justices oppose a certain precedent, that precedent survives. *Roe, Mapp,* and *Miranda* are three examples. There is something about being justices that restrains a majority of the Court from voting to overturn settled law.

To some degree, the justices are constrained by many of the factors identified earlier in the book: institutional weaknesses, lack of capacity, and the fact that the Court is undemocratic. In the final chapter, I combine the different institutional and individual perspectives to derive some conclusions about the nature and scope of the dilemma.

Notes

1. Even James Garfield, who was assassinated six months into his term had the opportunity to choose a Supreme Court justice.

2. The Court received widespread criticism for this decision. Within three years, the Court took the unusual step of reversing it.

3. In his concurring opinion, Justice Goldberg added the open-ended Ninth Amendment, which reads, "The enumeration in the Constitution, of certain rights, shall not be construed to deny or disparage others retained by the people."

4. The "legal realists," writing in the early twentieth century, were among the first to challenge the normative orthodoxy that justices followed a strict legal model and carefully weighed the laws and facts in each case before reaching a disinterested decision. The realists accepted the influence of a variety of different factors on decisionmaking.

5. Black, for instance, was an absolutist about free speech. He felt that there could be no restrictions on the spoken word. However, when it came to symbolic speech, such as wearing an armband or burning a draft card, Black was willing to permit governmental restrictions.

6. The story had a happy ending, but maybe not the happiest for Justice Hughes. He was defeated in his run for the presidency, but was reappointed to the Supreme Court as chief justice.

7

Toward Resolving the Dilemma: A Return to the Recent Past

I HAVE SPENT THE better part of this book examining the dilemma surrounding the appropriate role for the U.S. Supreme Court. On the face of it, there is a compelling case for the Court to limit its policymaking and to confine its authority to resolving individual cases. There are a number of reasons why the Court should adopt judicial restraint as its typical response: The justices are unelected, the judiciary has institutional limitations built into the Constitution, and the Court lacks the capacity to see its decisions carried into effect. In each chapter, though, there have been arguments for increased judicial power that also seemed strong. Ultimately, the issue can never be resolved conclusively one way or another. I want to use the last chapter to suggest a possible role for the Supreme Court that reflects the potential and limitations of the institution.

The Mysterious Branch of Government Nobody Knows

The Supreme Court is often referred to as the Marble Palace. The justices don robes and speak what seems to outsiders to be a foreign language. The nine justices are largely invisible to the outside world. The Court is a mystery, and the justices seem to like it that way. On an individual level, the justices are perhaps the most powerful people in Washington, D.C., who nobody knows. The institution and the extent of its power and authority are not well-known either

It turns out that to not know the Supreme Court is to love the Supreme Court. The Court is held in high regard by the public and generally by the elected branches that interact with the institution. Part of that respect stems from the fact that the public traditionally believes that the Court largely acts in a disinterested fashion, weighing the facts and paying attention to the Constitution and precedents.[1] In some ways, the justices are like nine Wizards of Oz: They hold quasi-religious, supernatural positions in our government and silently and implicitly offer the advice to "pay no attention to the men and women behind the curtain."

The Court holds a unique position relative to the other branches of government. The public does not hold Congress in high regard. This is not surprising. Members of Congress run for reelection by campaigning against their own institution, claiming it is filled with scoundrels and the voters should send them back to keep an eye on their colleagues (Fenno 1975). Public support for the presidency is relatively high, but support for individual presidents varies with the occupant of the West Wing.

The relative invisibility of the Court is no accident. The need to apply the law in an objective, evenhanded manner gives justices a legitimate reason to keep their deliberations and procedures from public view. The justices do not allow cameras into the Court for oral arguments, and they do not make it easy for the journalists who cover the institution to interpret decisions. For that matter, they take no extraordinary steps to ensure that lower court judges know of their rulings. As a result, it is not surprising that the role of the Court is unclear.

There is little public pressure brought to bear on the institution. If the Supreme Court adopts judicial restraint by adhering to precedent and following the elected branches of government, it would largely fly under the radar of most of the public. The Court and its members would remain invisible and noncontroversial. Judicial restraint normally begets judicial respect. Taken to an extreme, however, judicial restraint can incur its own costs. Persistent judicial restraint may create judicial abdication.

Activism, on the other hand, makes the Court a moving target and inhibits its ability to remain a coequal branch. When the Court becomes embroiled in the social conflicts of the day or weighs in on a presidential election, it grabs the attention of the public and the other branches and invites additional scrutiny and close monitoring (Wallace 1997, 168–169). By exercising judicial activism, the Court risks exposing its weaknesses and raises expectations that may exceed its capacity. Some consider judicial activism a form of disregard for the elected branches of government and claim the Court invites those seeking redress for their problems to make an end run of Congress in favor of a judicial remedy.

There are some compelling reasons and attractive forces that invite the Court to exercise activism. Certainly many provisions of the Constitution were drafted in general terms. According to Judge Richard Posner (1997, 184), "This creates flexibility in the face of unforeseen changes, but it also creates the possibility of multiple interpretations, and this possibility is an embarrassment for a theory of judicial legitimacy that denies that judges have any right to exercise discretion."

Some argue that only an outside force like the Supreme Court has the ability to make decisions that depart from standard procedures. Justices have the ability to act when other institutions will not because they do not have to face the voters and they have life tenure. Too often, the political branches seem to respond only to the voices of the powerful. The Court, on the other hand, provides access to the government for those who are excluded from the other branches.

The Court can use its position as a protector of minority rights and its moral authority to ensure that the elected branches of government limit the reach of their authority in civil liberties. Federal or state governments have passed enlightened laws that protect groups and individuals, but they also have passed laws that have restricted rights and liberties. The Supreme Court needs to be vigilant in those areas. As Perry (1982, 163) notes, "Constitutional policymaking by the judiciary has served the American polity as an agency of ongoing, insistent moral reevaluation and ultimately of moral growth."

The Supreme Court is a flawed institution. It was constructed that way by the framers. Despite the problems the Court faces, it has often been a very active policymaker. The normative idea that justices merely apply the law and never make the law is as unrealistic as the notion that the legislature acts only with "the consent of the governed" (Posner 1997, 184).

Recognizing the Constraints and Potential

In assuming the role of interpreting the Constitution and helping chart national public policy, the Court has been referred to as the "schoolmaster of the republic" (Franklin and Kosaki 1989). Some say the Supreme Court is "an educational body, and the Justices are inevitably teachers in a vital national seminar" (Funston 1978). As a result, the justices of the Court can be seen as the modern political theorists of the polity (Lowi 1968; Funston 1978). Their influence is further magnified if one places credence in adages that maintain, in effect, the justices determine what the Constitution actually means (Brigham 1987, 31). In helping to determine the scope of power granted the central government, the divisions between the three branches, the relationship of business to government, and the connections between the sociopolitical infrastructure and the economic system, the Court helps create an evolving vision of constitutional democracy.

More recently, the Court has assumed the dominant role in balancing the rights and liberties of individuals and minorities with the police powers of the government. The Court's attention to civil liberties and civil rights required the justices to breathe new life into the Bill of Rights and the Fourteenth Amendment. In constructing doctrine, the Court had to fashion a brand of political theory that would determine the nature of relationships between institutions and individuals.

Constitutional interpretation has undergone fundamental changes over time. *Brown v. Board of Education* was a major turning point. The Warren Court resuscitated judicial activism, after the post–New Deal passivity, but it was different from previous strains of activism. The Warren Court increasingly took the initiative in trying to engineer broad social reform, which led to controversy over whether its interpretation of the Constitution could be justified within acceptable canons of judicial practice. *Brown* was a symbol that justices were doing more than interpreting law, they were making law, fueling the growth of the so-called modern judicial activism.

The argument that the Constitution should change with the times is controversial. Remember, though, the Constitution recognized slavery and was written at a time when women had no political rights and men who did not own land were second-class citizens. Thus, there were reasons to hope some parts of the Constitution would change with the times. Even if individual provisions of the Constitution do not change, the tenor of the document could be adapted to the times. The desire for racial equality, reflected in *Brown*, signaled the transition of the Constitution and helped launch a renaissance for the Bill of Rights.[2] For much of the history of the Supreme Court and the nation, the Bill of Rights has been a catalog of platitudes and protections that the justices have never had the occasion to enforce to the fullest degree.

So how do we resolve the dilemma that faces the Supreme Court as an institution and the justices as individuals? The Supreme Court has some inherent weaknesses that limit its ability to move away from the acceptable boundaries established by public opinion and the elected branches of government. Lacking the "sword and the purse," the justices have to depend on the other branches of government to enforce their decisions, which is particularly problematic when the Court makes a sweeping decision that affects many people or definable groups. The modern Supreme Court has made a number of those types of decisions over the last half-century.

While the institutional limitations pose serious constraints, the Court has some reservoirs of power from which it can draw. Legitimacy, a finite resource to be sure, is a powerful symbolic force that the Court can draw upon when necessary. The Court has a great deal of diffuse support from the public, which means that the elected branches will be reluctant to attack it, even when there are unpopular decisions. It is difficult for the elected branches, whose members are often disdained as "politicians," to go after a quasi-religious institution that claims to speak for the Constitution.

If the Supreme Court works at the margins and adopts a position of judicial restraint, then it is unlikely to confront its institutional limitations. The Court runs the largest risks when it acts in an activist manner. Judicial activism occurs when the Court reverses the elected branches, "rewrites" portions of the Constitution, or makes sweeping decisions. Each of those aspects of judicial activism magnifies the institutional weaknesses of the Court.

There is another side to this coin, however. Would the Court sacrifice too much if it refused to act too often? Since *Brown*, the Court has been an active participant in public policymaking, particularly in the areas of civil rights and individual liberties. Now that the Court has ventured into these areas, it will be difficult to extricate itself. To close access would create intractable problems for certain groups. Similarly, certain issues are not suitable for the elected branches. There has long been the notion that individual rights, often reflected in the protection of unpopular groups, cannot adequately be protected by officeholders who have to face the voters every two, four, or six years.

One of the most troubling aspects of judicial policymaking is the fact that justices are unelected. The democratic arguments, however, are overblown in three respects. First, there is an undemocratic component to the Supreme Court that is built into the Constitution. The Court was designed to be undemocratic, though it did not fulfill the promise of that position until 1938, when it began to enunciate a role as the protector of insular minorities. Second, there are strong undemocratic elements in the elected branches: Congress is hardly an institution that is dominated by majoritarian sentiment. Incumbents are seemingly invulnerable, and interest groups have tremendous power. Presidents are not directly elected by the people, which became evident in 2000. Finally, there are democratic elements to the judicial process. Legal mobilization is a bottom-up phenomenon in which groups approach the Court, raising notions of pluralism. The democratization of the legal process has occurred in two directions: One, it allowed more groups access to the judiciary, and, two, specific protection of rights and liberties, such as speech and voting rights, was often directed at preserving and extending democracy to the disenfranchised.

The undemocratic nature of the Supreme Court moved from being a weakness of the institution to the reason for its existence: Once the Court had adopted the role as protector of insular minorities, it had a niche that no other branch of government could fulfill. As Leslie Goldstein (1995, 279) wrote, "Only a nonelected branch can reason and speak to the traditions and moral leadership necessary to make the nation better."

As always, there is another side to the issue. When the Court protects minorities and unpopular groups that have no recourse to the elected branches, it risks incurring the wrath of the public, Congress, and the president. Decisions that free a guilty person because of a police error or protect the rights of Nazis or Communists not only are undemocratic, but they raise the specter of the institutional weaknesses. If the other branches, or state officials, oppose Court decisions, there is a good chance that they will not faithfully implement them. This will expose the Court to the potential loss of legitimacy and raise concerns with judicial capacity.

The capacity argument rests on two different levels. On an absolute level, it does appear that a strong case can be made that the Court lacks the capacity to have its decisions carry the intended consequences. This is particularly problematic when the Supreme Court takes bold steps and makes sweeping public policy. The Court makes decisions on some of the most important and often difficult problems and offers its view of a solution. Seldom does the proposed solution work as planned, and often there will be unintended consequences. The bigger the issue, the less likely that the Court's decision will have the intended consequences.

The other level to the capacity argument is relative capacity. The Court has real problems, but it is not alone in that regard. Congress, the executive branch, and the bureaucracy, the alternative forums for policymakers, are constrained by their own capacity problems. Relatedly, the issues that expose the vulnerability of the Supreme Court are the intractable social problems that defy easy solutions, perhaps any solutions. Compounding the problems for the Court is the allegation that the elected branches, the supposedly ideal places for policymaking, ignore the difficult issues of the day—arguably because the members are elected and have to face the voters.

Maybe concern with capacity is misplaced. Perhaps it is more important that the Supreme Court does the right thing and does not worry about the ultimate prospects for the decision. The Court can add moral authority and transfer some of its legitimacy to the issue; when the Court throws its weight behind an issue, that may energize the public and the elected branches.

If the Court was to limit its role and adopt widespread judicial deference and restraint, it would avoid the problems attendant to judicial capacity. There would be consequences, however. It would mean that the Court would no longer serve as the protector of individual liberties and civil rights. Would another branch of government step into the vacuum? The prospects do not seem to be especially encouraging.

Designing a Role for the Supreme Court

The Court is supposed to be the voice of reason, charged with the creative function of articulating the durable principles of government. The normative view is that the justices should be governed by principles of constitutional law and statutory interpretation. The justices must respect the governmental structure and use reasoned principle and societal moral tradition, as well as history, the text of the Constitution, and judicial precedent as sources of inspiration. The justices need to pay attention to the broader context that Leslie Goldstein refers to as "the evolving morality of our tradition." Because the Court stands outside popular control, it should refrain from taking and deciding certain cases when it would be politically unwise. The justices need to find the underlying meaning embedded in the plans behind the Constitution. To deny the existence of broader guiding principles is to make the Court "a naked power organ" rather than a court of law (Goldstein 1995, 277–278).

In Chapter 2, I argued that since the late 1980s, the Supreme Court has begun to move away from the so-called double standard that dominated judicial decisionmaking for half a century. This move would help the Court resolve the dilemmas it faced. Part of the new role urges the Court to adopt judicial restraint when it deals with the actions of the elected branches. To do so would mitigate concerns that the Court is undemocratic. This new role also asks the Court to avoid making sweeping policy pronouncements. That would reduce concerns over the Court's institutional limitations and arguments about capacity. However, the adoption of such a role would represent an abdication of the role of the Court as a protector of minorities.

Despite its stated intentions, the Rehnquist Court has not been completely faithful to judicial restraint. Some charge that this Court stands the preferred position doctrine on its head. While the Court has tried to be faithful to restraint in civil liberties, it has exhibited significant activism in economic issues. The Rehnquist Court has resuscitated notions of economic due process, using the Takings Clause of the Fifth Amendment, revising federalism doctrine, and using the Commerce Clause as a means of scrutinizing economic regulations (Yarbrough 2000, 101–126). This book suggests that this is entirely the wrong role for the Court. The Court is actively involved in second-guessing the elected branches in economic matters, while it permits them to constrict civil liberties. Judicial activism in economic issues invites congressional retaliation. The abdication of civil liberties might well threaten the legitimacy of the Court.

Any role for the modern Supreme Court needs to include protection for the rights of minorities. Michael Perry (1982, 147) argues that the judiciary has a special duty to protect the "marginal" people of society. Rather than shrink from that role, the Court should embrace it, which means that the democratic dilemma should not be a deterrent for judicial decisionmaking in these areas. Indeed, footnote four of the *Carolene Products* decision is "perfectly consistent with Hamilton's description of the judiciary as a bulwark against majoritarian excesses, and with the language of the equal protection clause" (Justice 1997a, 159).

All of this suggests that the Court should readopt the double standard or preferred position doctrine. The Court would set itself up as *the* protector of individual liberties and civil rights by presuming that laws are unconstitutional and putting the burden on the state or federal government to prove otherwise; but the Court would respect the position of the elected branches in economic cases, meaning it would presume that economic laws are constitutional. The Court should adopt the same responses when the rules of access (standing, ripeness, mootness, and political questions) are involved. In enforcing or ignoring standing and political questions, the Court should be strict in economic issues and loosen the restraints in civil liberties questions.

By readopting the preferred position doctrine and staking out its territory as the primary protector of civil rights and individual liberties, the Court creates a role for itself that the other branches would need to respect. This would create a wider zone of legitimacy for the Court. Thus, in civil liberties and civil rights the Court would be recognized as the one branch of government with the authority and the insulation to make policy. There is another reason for the Court to be the dominant actor in this area: Most of the decisions in civil liberties involve interpretations of the Constitution, the province of the judiciary.

I will now return to the four examples of judicial activism identified in Chapter 1 to determine how this "new" role of the Court would affect them. The first two examples represent traditional forms of activism. The first example is overturning precedent. The Court should adhere to precedents that support civil liberties and civil rights and modify those that do not. The longer such precedents have existed, the more respect they should be accorded. The second example is aggressive use of judicial review. The term *double standard* holds the answer: Be vigilant and aggressive in using judicial review to protect insular minorities, but only exercise this prerogative in economic matters in the most extreme circumstances.

The modern forms of activism, statutory and constitutional interpretation, are more troubling. In statutory construction, the Court should err on the side of broader interpretation in civil rights and individual liberties. Congress can always overturn or modify such decisions. Most problematic are constitutional decisions that rewrite provisions or create broad remedies, because they are difficult to review or overturn without an amendment. The Court might well have to change the Constitution to reflect the times. The double standard not only permits but mandates changes to provisions dealing with civil liberties and civil rights. Even many of those who support activism, particularly under the double standard, urge restraint in the creation of broad remedies.

The Court is most justified in exercising these broad prerogatives when it is protecting civil rights or individual liberties. Such remedies should be used only when they reinforce decisions that are on firm constitutional or statutory grounds or when the Court is on the highest moral ground or has support from the neutral principles that undergird the Constitution. Even then, the Court should exercise this activism only after the elected branches have failed to act to support the decision.

How would this new role, which is a return to the recent past, fit with the constraints and limitations on the Supreme Court? Restraint in economic matters would recognize the institutional constraints on the Court. The elected branches, with their expert staff and bureaucracy, are better suited to determine economic matters. Activism in civil liberties is not overly problematic. Remember that civil liberties involve restrictions on governmental action. Such decisions tell the government that it cannot limit free speech or freedom of religion or admonish the police not to deny due process of law.

Avoiding economic issues would be consistent with democratic principles. Judicial activism in civil liberties and civil rights would run the risk of being undemocratic. For such issues, however, the democratic dilemma is a less relevant concern. Democracy and pluralism would be served by having one branch of government protect the rights of minorities. There has to be a brake on the excesses of democracy, and the Court is in the best position to provide that. This position would be further strengthened if the Court used its power to protect civil liberties in such a fashion as to ensure that the engines of democratic government run smoothly. In practical terms, this means the Court would take the greatest pains to protect voting rights and freedom of expression.

The expansive decisions and broad remedies would seem to cause the most potential problems. Some charge that footnote four opened the door for the broad activist remedies that get the Court in trouble, raising the specter of the institutional constraints. When the Court makes a sweeping pronouncement that requires active governmental intervention to implement, it is forced to rely on the other branches or the states. To create such remedies, the Court needs some authority, whether from the Constitution or neutral principles. The Court may need to pick its battles carefully to avoid overextending itself or to limit the number of fronts that it pursues.

Civil liberties issues, which ask the government to refrain from some restrictive activity, would not tend to implicate concerns with capacity. Civil rights, coupled with the imposition of broad remedies and attempts to make social policy, does raise the question of judicial capacity. In the end, intractable social problems defy any easy solution. The elected branches are no better suited to deal with these issues, and in some ways, they are less able and lack the will.

How would this be manifested in judicial decisionmaking? According to Goldstein (1995), there are three levels of authority for the American polity. The Constitution is the voice of the people and the highest authority. Unfortunately, constitutional provisions surrounding civil rights and civil liberties are among the least clear parts of the document.

The second level of authority is "constitutional politics—the ongoing dialogue between the people and the Supreme Court about the meaning of constitutional law." Constitutional politics would encompass the enduring values that underlie the Constitution, but it would also reflect an evolving sense of decency—suggesting that definitions of liberties and rights can change. While the notion of a

Constitution that changes with the times is troubling and seems to free the justices to exercise their own prerogatives, there are some advantages as well. Eighteenth-century notions of individual rights were very different from those that dominate the twenty-first century. Technology has changed the definition of free speech and freedom of the press, and the Court can mold the Constitution to reflect those changes.

The third level of authority gives great credence to the work of the legislative majorities of the moment. There are times, though, when the elected majority violates the provisions of the Constitution, and, in those instances, the Court can set aside legislative judgments. Only the Constitution is superior to the legislative majority. According to Goldstein (1995, 290), judicial review "is to be employed to guard the fruits of our better selves (constitutional rules) against the wishes of our lesser selves (preferences of mere legislative majorities)." Judge Richard Neely (1981, xiii) argues that courts alleviate "the most dangerous structural deficiencies of the other institutions of democratic government." Courts can provide a remedy for the excesses of democracy and bureaucratic routine. The least deference to the elected branches should come in civil liberties and civil rights cases.

How would this "new" judicial role translate to the individual level? Justices are supposed to rely on the words of the Constitution and the intent of the framers, yet these are the most obtuse in civil rights and individual liberties. This part of the Constitution should be most malleable. The standards of what constitutes cruel and unusual punishment, due process, and freedom of expression evolve with the times. A dynamic or changing Constitution is considered problematic because it allows the justices to use their own values and policy designs to determine what the provisions mean.

As noted, if the Constitution is unclear or original intent does not exist, there are still some enduring values or neutral principles than emanate from the document. If the justices can point to some broader philosophies, then it is not merely their ideological predilections that determine the outcome of the case. The justices can look to footnote four for a statement of general principles that could guide them.

Judges have had specialized training and socialization that advocates judicial restraint and presumably reduces the incentives for them to act in their own self-interest. Judges look to the Constitution because it is the expressed will of the people. Decisions will undoubtedly be colored by the justices' attitudes and their sense of justice, but those values need to be grounded in the text (Goldstein 1995, 288). The central principles of the constitutionally established nation, rather than the personal philosophies of the justices, should guide the exercise of judicial review.

THIS JUST IN, UNCONFIRMED SOURCES REPORT THAT
THE SUPREME COURT IS SELECTING THE NEXT POPE.

Figure 7.1   It couldn't come to this, could it? Cartoon by Laura Gunther.

Unfortunately, it is not that simple. As Judge Neely (1982, 26) notes, "Courts are the final arbiters of what the federal and state constitutions mean, and since every conceivable political question can theoretically be stated in constitutional terms (usually within the confines of the vague 'due process' or 'equal protection' clauses), courts essentially can define their own role in the political structure." It is worth remembering that the elder Justice John Marshall Harlan, who dissented in *Plessy v. Ferguson*, argued that the "Constitution does not confer on courts blanket authority to step into every situation where the political branch may be thought to have fallen short" (O'Brien 1997, 137).

There are few mechanisms for restricting the justices from judicial activism. The most prevalent, if least reliable, mechanism is judicial self-restraint: The justices have to establish their own limits. If the justices were to exercise judicial self-restraint in economic cases, as part of the role established under footnote four, that would entail deference to the elected branches of government, enforcement of the rules of access, and a narrow decision when the Court had to issue a ruling. However, in its treatment of individual liberties and civil rights cases, the Court should adopt judicial activism. That should be manifested by a skepticism of the policies of the elected branches, a willingness to ignore the rules of access, and a flexible interpretation of the provisions of the Bill of Rights.

In the end, the Supreme Court cannot save the nation, but perhaps it can buy time until the elected branches can fulfill their responsibilities (Miller 1982a, 186). By protecting civil liberties and civil rights and using judicial activism to ensure that public debate is robust, voting rights are respected, and the channels to the elected branches remain open and unencumbered, the Supreme Court can protect minority rights and enhance the legitimacy of the other branches of government.

I will leave the final word on this matter to Justice Benjamin Cardozo, who argued that the danger that the courts may come to oppress the public and political branches of government "must be balanced against those of independence from all restraint, independence on the part of public officials elected for brief terms, without the guiding force of a continuous tradition. On the whole, I believe the latter dangers to be the more formidable of the two" (Justice 1997a, 161).

Protecting the Court's Legitimacy

I started this book with a discussion of *Bush v. Gore,* and as I conclude the final chapter, it is worth revisiting one of the questions posed at the end of the Introduction: Would *Bush v. Gore* become a self-inflicted wound that permanently harms the Supreme Court? While the decision may have been justified on some grounds and provided some closure to the controversy and some legitimacy for George Bush, it also stopped a recount, arguably taking the decision from the voters. Indeed, the Court lost some public support, but given the visibility of the case, the partisan wrangling, and the close national vote, it was surprising that the decline was so small.[3]

The legitimacy of the Court is its most important resource. As long as the Court is perceived to be fulfilling its role, it will retain its authority. The risk is that the Court will overstep its boundaries. The Court has been on the threshold several times and paid for its aggressiveness on a few occasions. However, the passions of the moment pass, and the Court typically recovers. It has enjoyed enough respect historically and has enough allies to cushion its descent.

It is unlikely that *Bush v. Gore* alone will have a lasting negative impact on the Court as an institution. However, if the Court follows it with a number of controversial and unpopular decisions, exercises activism with sweeping decisions that change the Constitution, or acts beyond its capacity, it risks fulfilling the prophesy of those who predict a decline in its public support. The activism of the Rehnquist Court, in dramatic contradiction to its stated objectives, may continue to lead the judicial branch into dangerous straits.

The television cameras that surrounded the Court in December 2000, as the justices wrestled with the case, shone blinding lights into the Court's chambers.

Bush v. Gore demystified the Court and opened it to public scrutiny to an unprecedented degree. Given that some of the Court's legitimacy is tied to the aura surrounding it and the lack of public awareness, increased attention could have its costs. It could lead the Court to withdraw further behind the curtains that shroud the Court literally and figuratively.

Bush v. Gore may have short-term effects. The heightened furor tied to the Court's decision died down within a few months. However, external forces could still "wave the bloody shirt" in an attempt to keep the issue alive. It could be raised by Senate Democrats if a justice resigns and President Bush has to consider possible nominees. It could flare if Bush suffers problems that call his ability to govern into question. There might be internal provocation as well. Will a justice cite the decision as precedent in some future case, calling attention to the dispute once again? To this point, the justices, particularly those in the minority, have tried to mend the institution's public image. The justices have taken great pains to claim that the Court was engaged in a legitimate judicial act, rather than a questionable political one (Greenhouse 2001).

In the end, the public goes on with daily life, the hot rhetoric cools, and the Court resumes its traditional position in the governmental structure. The Court tempers its decisions, and the justices keep a lower profile. The Court bides its time, heals its wounds, and rebuilds its finite resources. The Court's short-term authority and long-term legitimacy depend in no small part on how it continues to resolve the ongoing dilemma that is the subject of this book.

Notes

1. A number of polls even after *Bush v. Gore* showed that a majority of those surveyed felt the justices acted on impartial grounds.

2. In the wake of *Brown*, the Supreme Court moved in many directions to extend civil rights. Free speech was expanded to protect blacks and civil rights workers in the South. The incorporation of the criminal procedure provisions of the Bill of Rights (applying the Bill of Rights to the states), like search and seizure under the Fourth Amendment, were part of a broad-based plan to protect African American defendants (Walker 1990; Powe 2000).

3. It is hard to compare polls because they ask different questions. However, an examination of a whole range of polls before and after the Supreme Court's intervention showed that fewer people had strong confidence in the Court and more had very little confidence, but the declines were not overwhelming. About a third of the public thinks politics plays a major role in judicial decision, about the same percentage thinks it plays somewhat of a role, and about 30 percent think it plays no role.

References

Abraham, Henry. 1999. *Justices, presidents, and senators.* Revised edition. Lanham, Md.: Rowman and Littlefield.

Aldisert, Ruggero. 1997. The role of courts in contemporary society. In *Judges on judging: Views from the bench.* Edited by David O'Brien. Chatham, N.J.: Chatham House.

Aldrich, John. 1994. Rational choice theory and the study of American politics. In *The dynamics of American politics: Approaches and interpretations.* Edited by Lawrence Dodd and Calvin Jillson. Boulder: Westview Press.

Bamberger, Michael. 2000. *Reckless legislation: How lawmakers ignore the Constitution.* New Brunswick, N.J.: Rutgers University Press.

Bartee, Alice Fleetwood. 1984. *Cases lost, causes won.* New York: St. Martin's.

Baugh, Joyce Ann, Christopher Smith, Thomas Hensley, and Scott Patrick Johnson. 1994. Justice Ruth Bader Ginsburg: A preliminary assessment. *University of Toledo Law Review* 26: 1–34.

Baum, Lawrence. 1989. Comparing the policy positions of Supreme Court justices from different periods. *Western Political Quarterly* 42: 509–522.

———. 1997. *The puzzle of judicial behavior.* Ann Arbor: University of Michigan Press.

———. 2001. *The Supreme Court.* 6th ed. Washington D.C.: Congressional Quarterly.

Baumgartner, Frank, and Bryan Jones. 1993. *Agendas and instability in American politics.* Chicago: University of Chicago Press.

Berger, Raoul. 1977. *Government by judiciary.* Cambridge, Mass.: Harvard University Press.

Bickel, Alexander. 1962. *The least dangerous branch: The Supreme Court at the bar of politics.* Indianapolis, Ind.: Bobbs-Merrill.

———. 1975. *The morality of consent.* New Haven: Yale University Press.

Bork, Robert. 1990. *The tempting of America: The political seduction of the law.* New York: Free Press.

Brennan, William. 1986. The Constitution of the United States: Contemporary ratification. *South Texas Law Review* 27: 433–445.

———. 1987. Interpreting the Constitution. *Social Policy* 18: 24–28.

Brigham, John. 1987. *The cult of the Court.* Philadelphia: Temple University Press.

Canon, Bradley. 1991. Courts and policy compliance, implementation, and impact. In *The American courts: A critical assessment,* edited by John Gates and Charles Johnson. Washington, D.C.: Congressional Quarterly.

Caplan, Lincoln. 1987. *The tenth justice.* New York: Vintage Books.

Casper, Jonathan. 1976. The Supreme Court and national policy making. *American Political Science Review* 70: 50–63.

Cavanagh, Ralph, and Austin Sarat. 1980. Thinking about courts: Toward and beyond a jurisprudence of judicial competence. *Law and Society Review* 14: 371–419.

Chayes, Abram. 1976. The role of the judge in public law litigation. *Harvard Law Review* 89: 1281–1316.

Cheney, Timothy. 1998. *Who makes the law: The Supreme Court, Congress, the states, and society.* Upper Saddle River, N.J.: Prentice-Hall.

Choper, Jesse. 1980. *Judicial review and the national political process: A functional reconsideration of the role of the Supreme Court.* Chicago: University of Chicago Press.

Cortner, Richard. 1970. *The apportionment cases.* Knoxville: University of Tennessee Press.

_____. 1981. *The Supreme Court and the second bill of rights.* Madison: University of Wisconsin Press.

Cox, Archibald. 1976. *The role of the American Supreme Court in American government.* New York: Oxford University Press.

Dahl, Robert. 1957. Decision-making in a democracy: The Supreme Court as a national policy-maker. *Journal of Public Law* 6: 279–295.

Davidson, Roger, and Walter Oleszek. 1997. *Congress and its members.* 6th ed. Washington, D.C.: Congressional Quarterly.

Devins, Neal. 1996. *Shaping constitutional values: Elected government, the Supreme Court, and the abortion dilemma.* Baltimore: Johns Hopkins University Press.

Downing, Ronald. 1970. Judicial ethics and the political role of the courts. *Law and Contemporary Problems* 35: 94–107.

Ducat, Craig. 1978. *Modes of constitutional interpretation.* Minneapolis: West Publishing.

Dunn, William. 1981. *An introduction to public policy analysis.* Engelwood Cliffs, N.J.: Prentice-Hall.

Eisler, Kim Isaac. 1993. *A justice for all: William J. Brennan Jr. and the decisions that transformed America.* New York: Simon and Schuster.

Ely, James. 1992. *The guardian of every other right.* New York: Oxford University Press.

Epp, Charles. 1998. *The rights revolution: Lawyers, activists, and Supreme Courts in comparative perspective.* Chicago: University of Chicago Press.

Epstein, Lee, and Jack Knight. 1998. *The choices justices make.* Washington, D.C.: CQ Press.

Epstein, Lee, and Joseph Kobylka. 1992. *The Supreme Court and legal change: Abortion and the death penalty.* Chapel Hill: University of North Carolina Press.

Epstein, Lee, and Thomas Walker. 1998a. *Constitutional law for a changing America: Institutional powers and constraints.* 3d ed. Washington, D.C.: Congressional Quarterly.

_____. 1998b. *Constitutional law for a changing America: Rights, liberties and justice.* 3d ed. Washington, D.C.: Congressional Quarterly.

Eskridge, William. 1994. *Dynamic statutory interpretation.* Cambridge, Mass.: Harvard University Press.

The Federalist Papers. See Alexander Hamilton et al.

Fenno, Richard. 1975. If, as Ralph Nader says, "Congress is the broken branch," how come we love our congressmen so much? In *Congress in change,* edited by Norman Ornstein. New York: Praeger.

Fisher, Louis. 1988. *Constitutional dialogues: Interpretation as political process.* Princeton, N.J.: Princeton University Press.

Flemming, Roy, John Bohte, and B. Dan Wood. 1997. One voice among many: The Supreme Court's influence on attentiveness to issues in the U.S., 1947–1992. *American Journal of Political Science* 41: 1224–1250.

Franklin, Charles, and Liane Kosaki. 1989. Republican schoolmaster: The U.S. Supreme Court, public opinion, and abortion. *American Political Science Review* 83: 751–771.

Funston, Richard. 1975. The Supreme Court and critical elections. *American Political Science Review* 69: 795–811.

_____. 1978. *A vital national seminar: The Supreme Court in American political life.* Palo Alto, Calif.: Mayfield.

Galanter, Marc. 1974. Why the "haves" come out ahead: Speculations on the limits of legal change. *Law and Society Review* 9: 95–160.

Gambitta, Richard A.L., Marilyn L. May, and James C. Foster. 1981. *Governing through courts.* Beverly Hills, Calif.: Sage.

Gates, John. 1992. *The Supreme Court and partisan realignment.* Boulder: Westview Press.

Gillman, Howard. 1993. *The Constitution beseiged: The rise and demise of Lochner era police powers jurisprudence.* Durham, N.C.: Duke University Press.

Goldman, Sheldon, and Thomas Jahnige. 1985. *The federal courts as a political system.* 3d ed. New York: Harper and Row.

Goldstein, Leslie Friedman. 1991. *In defense of the text: Democracy and constitutional theory.* Savage, Md.: Rowman and Littlefield.

_____. 1995. By consent of the governed: Directions in constitutional theory. In *Contemplating courts,* edited by Lee Epstein. Washington, D.C.: Congressional Quarterly.

Graham, Hugh Davis. 1990. *The civil rights era: Origins and development of national policy 1960–1972.* New York: Oxford University Press.

Greenhouse, Linda. 2001. Election case a test and a trauma for justices. *New York Times.* February 20.

Halpern, Stephen. 1995. *On the limits of the law: The ironic legacy of Title VI of the 1964 Civil Rights Act.* Baltimore: Johns Hopkins University Press.

Hamilton, Alexander, James Madison, and John Jay. 1981. *The Federalist Papers,* edited by Roy Fairfield. 2d ed. Baltimore: Johns Hopkins University Press.

Hausegger, Lori, and Lawrence Baum. 1999. Inviting congressional action: A study of Supreme Court motivations in statutory interpretation. *American Journal of Political Science* 43: 162–183.

Heath, Jim. 1975. *Decade of disillusionment: The Kennedy-Johnson years.* Bloomington: Indiana University Press.

Heclo, Hugh. 1978. Issue networks and the executive establishment. In *The new American system,* edited by Anthony King. Washington, D.C.: American Enterprise Institute.

Hickok, Eugene, and Gary McDowell. 1993. *Justice vs. law: Courts and politics in American society.* New York: Free Press.

Hoff, Joan. 1991. *Law, gender, and injustice: A legal history of U.S. women.* New York: New York University Press.

Horowitz, Donald. 1977. *The courts and social policy.* Washington, D.C.: Brookings.

Irons, Peter. 1990. *The courage of their convictions.* New York: Penguin Books.

Jackson, Robert. 1997. The Supreme Court in the American system of government. In *Judges on judging: Views from the bench,* edited by David O'Brien. Chatham, N.J.: Chatham House.

Johnson, Charles, and Bradley Canon. 1999. *Judicial policies: Implementation and impact.* 2d ed. Washington, D.C.: Congressional Quarterly.

Justice, William Wayne. 1997a. A relativistic Constitution. In *Judges on judging: Views from the bench,* edited by David O'Brien. Chatham, N.J.: Chatham House.

————. 1997b. The two faces of judicial activism. In *Judges on judging: Views from the bench,* edited by David O'Brien. Chatham, N.J.: Chatham House.

Kahn, Ronald. 1994. *The Supreme Court and constitutional theory, 1953–1993.* Lawrence: University Press of Kansas.

Kingdon, John. 1989. *Congressmen's voting decisions.* 3d ed. Ann Arbor: University of Michigan Press.

————. 1995. *Agendas, alternatives, and public policies.* 2d ed. Boston: Little, Brown.

Kutler, Stanley. 1984. *The Supreme Court and the Constitution.* 3d ed. New York: W. W. Norton.

Lawson, Kay. 1993. *The human polity: A comparative introduction to political science.* 3d ed. Boston: Houghton-Mifflin.

Lindgren, J. Ralph, and Nadine Taub. 1993. *The law of sex discrimination.* 2d ed. Minneapolis: West Publishing.

Lowi, Theodore. 1968. *The end of liberalism.* New York: Norton.

————. 1979. *The end of liberalism.* 2d ed. New York: Norton.

Maltz, Earl. 2000. *The chief justiceship of Warren Burger, 1969–1986.* Columbia: University of South Carolina Press.

Mason, Alpheus Thomas. 1979. *The Supreme Court from Taft to Burger.* Baton Rouge: Louisiana State University Press.

Mayhew, David. 1974. *Congress: The electoral connection.* New Haven: Yale University Press.

McCann, Michael. 1994. *Rights at work: Pay equity reform and the politics of legal mobilization.* Chicago: University of Chicago Press.

McCloskey, Robert. 1960. *The American Supreme Court.* Chicago: University of Chicago Press.

McConnell, Grant. 1966. *Private power and American capitalism.* New York: Knopf.

McCubbins, Matthew, and Thomas Schwartz. 1984. Congressional oversight overlooked: Police patrols versus fire alarms. *American Journal of Political Science* 28: 167–179.

McDowell, Gary. 1982. *Equity and the Constitution.* Chicago: University of Chicago Press.

McKeever, Robert. 1993. *Raw judicial power? The Supreme Court and American society.* New York: Manchester University Press.

Meese, Edwin. 1985. The attorney general's view of the Supreme Court: Toward a jurisprudence of original intent. *Public Administration Review* 45: 701–704.

Miller, Arthur Selwyn. 1982a. In defense of judicial activism. In *Supreme Court activism and restraint,* edited by Stephen Halpern and Charles Lamb. Lexington, Ky.: Heath.

————. 1982b. *Toward increased judicial activism.* Westport, Conn.: Greenwood Press.

Murphy, Walter, James Fleming, and William Harris II. 1986. *American constitutional interpretation*. Mineola, N.Y.: Foundation Press.

Murphy, Walter, and Joseph Tanenhaus. 1968. Public opinion and the United States Supreme Court. *Law and Society Review* 2: 357–384.

Neely, Richard. 1981. *How courts govern America*. New Haven: Yale University Press.

_____. 1982. *Why courts don't work*. New York: McGraw-Hill.

Neustadt, Richard. 1976. *Presidential power: The politics of leadership with reflections on Johnson and Nixon*. New York: John Wiley and Sons.

Newmyer, R. Kent. 1968. *The Supreme Court under Marshall and Taney*. New York: Crowell.

O'Brien, David, ed. 1997. *Judges on judging: Views from the bench*. Chatham, N.J.: Chatham House.

_____. 2000. *Storm center: The Supreme Court in American politics*. New York: Norton.

Pacelle, Richard. 1991. *The Transformation of the Supreme Court's agenda: From the New Deal to the Reagan administration*. Boulder: Westview Press.

_____. 1995. The dynamics and determinants of agenda change in the Rehnquist Court. In *Contemplating courts*, edited by Lee Epstein. Washington, D.C.: Congressional Quarterly.

Peltason, Jack. 1961. *Fifty-eight lonely men: Southern federal judges and school desegregation*. Urbana: University of Illinois Press.

Perry, H. W. 1991. *Deciding to decide: Agenda setting in the United States Supreme Court*. Cambridge, Mass.: Harvard University Press.

Perry, Michael. 1982. *The Constitution, the courts, and human rights*. New Haven: Yale University Press.

Posner, Richard. 1997. What am I a potted plant? The case against strict constructionism. In *Judges on judging: Views from the bench*, edited by David O'Brien. Chatham, N.J.: Chatham House.

Powe, Lucas. 2000. *The Warren Court and American politics*. Cambridge, Mass.: Bellknap Press.

Pritchett, C. Herman. 1954. *Civil liberties and the Vinson Court*. Chicago: University of Chicago Press.

_____. 1984a. *Constitutional civil liberties*. Englewood Cliffs, N.J.: Prentice-Hall.

_____. 1984b. *Constitutional law of the federal system*. Englewood Cliffs, N.J.: Prentice-Hall.

Rehnquist, William. 1997. The notion of a living Constitution. In *Judges on judging: Views from the bench*, edited by David O'Brien. Chatham, N.J.: Chatham House.

Riley, Dennis. 1987. *Controlling the federal bureaucracy*. Philadelphia: Temple University Press.

Ripley, Randall, and Grace Franklin. 1982. *Bureaucracy and policy implementation*. Homewood, Ill.: Dorsey Press.

_____. 1990. *Congress, the bureaucracy, and public policy*. 5th ed. Homewood, Ill.: Dorsey Press.

Rosenberg, Gerald. 1991. *The hollow hope: Can courts bring about social change?* Chicago: University of Chicago Press.

Savage, David. 1992. *Turning right: The making of the Rehnquist Court.* New York: Wiley.

Schattschneider, E. E. 1975. *The semisovereign people: A realist's view of democracy in America.* Hinsdale, Ill.: Dryden Press.

Schwartz, Bernard. 1983. *Super Chief: Earl Warren and his Supreme Court—A judicial biography.* New York: New York University Press.

———. 1990. *The ascent of pragmatism: The Burger Court in action.* Reading, Pa.: Addison-Wesley Publishing.

———. 1993. *A history of the Supreme Court.* New York: Oxford University Press.

———. 1998. The Burger Court in action. In *The Burger Court: Counter-revolution or confirmation?* edited by Bernard Schwartz. New York: Oxford University Press.

Segal, Jeffrey, and Harold Spaeth. 1993. *The Supreme Court and the attitudinal model.* New York: Cambridge University Press.

Shafritz, Jay. 1992. *The Harper Collins dictionary of American government and politics.* New York: HarperPerennial.

Sickels, Robert. 1988. *John Paul Stevens and the Constitution: The search for balance.* University Park: Pennsylvania State University Press.

Silverstein, Mark. 1983. *Constitutional faiths.* Ithaca: Cornell University Press.

Simon, James. 1995. *The center holds: The power struggle inside the Rehnquist Court.* New York: Simon and Schuster.

Smith, Christopher. 1997. *Courts, politics, and the judicial process.* 2d ed. Chicago: Nelson-Hall.

Smith, Martin. 1993. *Pressure power and policy: State autonomy and policy networks in Britain and the United States.* Pittsburgh: University of Pittsburgh Press.

Smith, Rogers. 1985. *Liberalism and American constitutional law.* Cambridge, Mass.: Harvard University Press.

Spaeth, Harold. 1995. The attitudinal model. In *Contemplating courts,* edited by Lee Epstein. Washington, D.C.: Congressional Quarterly.

Sundquist, James. 1968. *Politics and policy: The Eisenhower, Kennedy, and Johnson years.* Washington, D.C.: Brookings Institution.

———. 1983. *Dynamics of the party system: Alignment and realignment of political parties in the United States.* Revised ed. Washington, D.C.: Brookings Institution.

Tribe, Laurence. 1985. *Constitutional choices.* Cambridge, Mass.: Harvard University Press.

Urofsky, Melvin. 1991. *The continuity of change: The Supreme Court and individual liberties, 1953–1986.* Belmont, Calif.: Wadsworth.

Wahlbeck, Paul. 1997. The life of the law: Judicial politics and legal change. *Journal of Politics* 59: 778–802.

Walker, Samuel. 1990. *In defense of American liberties: A history of the ACLU.* New York: Oxford University Press.

Walker, Thomas, Lee Epstein, and William Dixon. 1988. On the mysterious demise of consensual norms in the United States Supreme Court. *Journal of Politics* 50: 361–389.

Wallace, J. Clifford. 1997. The jurisprudence of judicial restraint: A return to the moorings. In *Judges on judging: Views from the bench,* edited by David O'Brien. Chatham, N.J.: Chatham House.

Wasby, Stephen. 1984. *The Supreme Court in the federal judicial system.* 2d ed. New York: Holt, Rinehart, and Winston.

_____. 1995. *Race relations litigation in an age of complexity.* Charlottesville: University of Virginia Press.

Wechsler, Herbert. 1959. Toward neutral principles of constitutional law. *Harvard Law Review* 73: 1–35.

Witt, Elder. 1981. *The Supreme Court and its work.* Washington, D.C.: Congressional Quarterly.

_____. 1990. *Guide to the Supreme Court, 2d Ed.,* Washington, D.C.: Congressional Quarterly.

_____. 1986. *A different justice.* Washington, D.C.: Congressional Quarterly.

Wolfe, Christopher. 1997. *Judicial activism: Bulwark of freedom or precarious security?* Lanham, Md.: Rowman and Littlefield.

Yarbrough, Tinsley. 2000. *The Rehnquist Court and the Constitution.* New York: Oxford University Press.

Youngblood, J. Craig, and Parker Folse III. 1981. Can courts govern? An inquiry into capacity. In *Governing through courts,* edited by Richard A. L. Gambitta, Marilyn L. May, and James C. Foster. Beverly Hills, Calif.: Sage.

About the Author

Richard Pacelle is Associate Professor of Political Science and Legal Studies Coordinator at the University of Missouri, St. Louis. He received his Ph.D. from Ohio State University. Professor Pacelle teaches constitutional law, civil liberties, judicial process, American politics, and methodology, as well as judicial decisionmaking—a simulation of the United States Supreme Court. He is the recipient of the 2000-2001 Chancellor's Award for Teaching Excellence and the 2000–2001 Governor's Award for Teaching Excellence. Professor Pacelle is the author of *The Transformation of the Supreme Court's Agenda: From the New Deal to the Reagan Administration (1991)* and *Between Law and Politics: The Solicitor General and the Structuring of Race, Gender, and Reproductive Rights Policy* (forthcoming) and a number of articles and book chapters.

Index